From Colonialism to the Contemporary

From Colonialism to the Contemporary: Intertextual Transformation in World Children's and Youth Literature

Edited By

Lance Weldy

CAMBRIDGE
SCHOLARS

P U B L I S H I N G

From Colonialism to the Contemporary: Intertextual Transformation in World Children's and Youth Literature, Edited by Lance Weldy

This book first published 2006. The present binding first published 2009.

Cambridge Scholars Publishing

12 Back Chapman Street, Newcastle upon Tyne, NE6 2XX, UK

British Library Cataloguing in Publication Data
A catalogue record for this book is available from the British Library

ISBN (10): 1-4438-0519-X, ISBN (13): 978-1-4438-0519-3

TABLE OF CONTENTS

INTRODUCTION

The compilation of this book has been carefully constructed to convey the essence of its title, *From Colonialism to the Contemporary: Intertextual Transformation in World Children's and Youth Literature*. In other words, the different chapters have been selected and ordered to illustrate the chronological effects surrounding the phenomenon of Children's and Youth Literature. While this selection of essays as a whole does not seek to provide an exhaustive historical analysis of literature surrounding and written for children, it does seek to highlight several points in time that will give the reader a sound understanding of certain shifts in ideology found in children's literature. For example, to illustrate how the strikingly prevalent, hegemonic nature of colonialism bridged across the Atlantic Ocean from the U.K. to the U.SA., Tammy Mielke contributes her chapter, "Transforming a Stereotype: *Little Black Sambo*'s American Illustrators," which discusses how the racial tension and controversy surrounded the phenomenon of the popular picture book written in 1898. Making reference to the child's identity as a colonized subject, Mielke traces the rocky start of this book's first publication and how the illustrations through the decades have transformed to mirror the ideologies of the respective publishers. Her chapter gives a good indication of how the representation of the African American child transformed during the first few decades of the 20th century.

But the movement from colonialism to contemporary ideology is not the only transformation involved in our series of essays. This anthology also focuses on innovative and postmodern elements in works for and about children. As Elina Druker's chapter, "Images within Images in Tove Jansson's Picturebooks," illustrates, the manner in which the story is transmitted to the child can be transformed by experimenting with spatiality in picture books. Her in-depth analysis of Tove Jannson's books from the 1940's and 50's reveals the innovative creativity of texts in the vein of Randolph Caldecott's mastery of relationship between text and picture. In essence, one aspect of Druker's essay focuses on the *intra*textuality of Jansson's picture books.

The last four chapters of this book focus on how well-known works for or about children have been revised or updated for the early 21st century. The original texts range from those spoken or written from ancient times to oral and written tales from two centuries ago. Regardless of the historicity of the original texts being updated, these essays specialize in the intertextual nature and special relationship conveyed between the past and the contemporary. Another way of conveying this notion is to say that these chapters are not only looking at the transformative aspect of their updated texts, but also how this transformative aspect responds to the intertextuality inherent in the revising. Beth Cooley's chapter, "Jerry Spinelli's *Stargirl* as Contemporary Gospel," analyzes perhaps the best-known story in the western hemisphere—the story of Jesus Christ—and shows how Spinelli's text transfers the original gospel story onto a high school campus. Cooley highlights the postmodern elements that make this a contemporary gospel, most notably how the typological Christ figure is an avant-garde school girl.

The next two chapters focus on updated versions of fairy tales, and while the well-known genesis of fairy tales stems from oral tales from respective cultures, these two chapters look at the early written sources of tales from such well-known names as the Brothers Grimm and Charles Perrault. Debra Mitts-Smith looks at the cultural concept of the wolf and the shift in perception about this representative of evil. Her chapter, "Rehabilitating the Wolf: Intertextuality and Visual Allusion in Geoffrey de Pennart's Picture Books," follows not only the intertextual, transformative nature of de Pennart's updated picture books, but also the intertextual relationship within his series of books that follow the story of a few generations of wolves from various well-known fairy tales. While Mitts-Smith works with the cultural perception of the wolf, Lance Weldy's chapter, "Once Upon a Time in Idaho: Transforming Cinderella through A-temporality, Awkwardness, and Adolescence in *Napoleon Dynamite*," looks at the popular indie hit movie within the lens of arguably the most popular fairy tale, "Cinderella." In Weldy's essay, the original "Cinderella" tale becomes scrutinized in order to better understand the reason behind the popularity of *Napoleon Dynamite*. Essentially, Weldy argues that the rhetorical attraction of this film is *Dynamite*'s ability to update the "Cinderella" tale for a postmodern audience.

Finally, the last chapter concludes this study with a look at one of the most recent examples of cultural transformation in a world text. In this case, it relates to the concept of a hero. Sara Crabtree's essay, "Harry the Hero? The Quest for Self-Identity, Heroism, and Transformation in the *Goblet of Fire*," scrutinizes the worldwide phenomenon of *Harry Potter* within the constructs of a classical and contemporary hero. Through a postmodern lens, Crabtree argues for the legitimate potential for Harry to be a hero, not of a classical nature, but of an updated kind that allows for an individual's foibles. A secondary focus of her essay is exploring the relationship and nature between the book and currently released film, *Harry Potter and the Goblet of Fire*.

As the summary of these chapters demonstrate, the focus of this book is multivalent and interconnecting. While historically tracing a few texts from around the world along a timeline, this book also seeks to convey the transformative and intertextual nature of these respective texts, thereby revealing that children's literature is not an isolated genre, but instead one that conveys—and is subject to—all the same ideologies as other genres of literature. Furthermore, it is important to note that these chapters highlight texts from around the world, as the title expresses. Therefore, the reader can see how audiences have responded to and transformed texts pertaining to such countries and regions as India, Western Europe, Scandinavia, the United Kingdom, and the United States. Meta-narratively speaking, this book also reflects the multinational nature and audience of this book as well, with contributing scholars writing from and representing various parts of the world. Most importantly, I want to point out that the thread that ties all of these topics together is Transformation.

I do want to make one last small comment about our book's title, specifically the last portion, because in my brief career in the academic world of Children's Literature, I have noticed the potentially volatile semantics when seeking to categorize the kind of literature explored within this book.

In some sectors of this field of study, "Children's Literature" is regarded as texts geared primarily towards those children aged 0 to 6, 7, or even 8—essentially early primary grades. On the other end of the spectrum, scholars use this very same title to envelop all texts up to the early young adult ages. Incidentally, this difficulty in a universal categorizing of texts also spills over into these very texts written for the older audience, leaving certain textbooks or scholars to use terminology such as "Adolescent" or "Young Adult," each of which may encapsulate a different range of ages. Ultimately, I have chosen the title "Children's and Youth Literature" to express that this book covers texts for both younger children, as in Geoffroy de Pennart's books and perhaps even *Napoleon Dynamite;* and older children, such as *Goblet of Fire* and *Stargirl*, and it is my hope that this book will express the excitement and attraction that we as Children's Literature scholars have and feel for these representative texts.

Lance Weldy, Ph.D., editor
Fulbright Fellow
Johann Wolfgang Goethe Universität
Frankfurt am Main

CHAPTER ONE

TRANSFORMING A STEREOTYPE: *LITTLE BLACK SAMBO*'S AMERICAN ILLUSTRATORS

TAMMY MIELKE

"What's past is prologue."
-William Shakespeare, *The Tempest*

[*Editor's note*: The material in this article comes from a much larger dissertation chapter, *Tom, Sambo, and Remus: Early Literary Constructs in books Constructing African American Childhood*. For the purposes of this book, this chapter will only focus on the phenomenon surrounding Helen Bannerman's *Little Black Sambo*.]

The function of this chapter is to provide analysis of one major literary aspect—illustration—which was utilised by authors and illustrators to build literary constructs of African American childhood before the 1930s. Through the use of characterisation in the changing use of illustration in the various versions of *The Story of Little Black Sambo* (1898) by Helen Bannerman, the early versions of literary constructions of African American childhood in the 1930s are deciphered. While this thesis is centred on literature produced during the 1930s and about the 1930s, these early constructs serve as foundations for later constructs of African American childhood.

Researching the historical content and background of minority literature is fundamental in understanding the development of that minority literature. The postcolonial critic Abdul JanMohamed observed, "archival work is essential to the critical articulation of the minority discourse."[1] In keeping with JanMohamed's observation, this chapter reveals early constructs of African American childhood in American children's literature which later influenced the constructs of African American childhood in the 1930s.

---

[1] Abdul JanMohamed, ed., *The Nature and Context of Minority Discourse* (New York: Oxford University Press, 1990), 5.

Little Black Sambo (1898) was chosen because of its popularity both at the time produced and today, which tends to invoke intense discussion in the United States[2] between critics, educators, and parents about race and literature. It has never gone out of publication in spite of the plethora of negative criticisms and doctored illustrations. Bannerman's divisive book rates number ninety on the Most Banned Book list for 1990-1999 (ALA) even though it has been over one hundred years since its first publication.

The subject of this thesis specifies that the literature under consideration must be "American Children's Literature." This wording predetermines two specific aspects: the literature must be American and the literature must be intended for a child, i.e. non-adult, audience. The inclusion of *Little Black Sambo* might seem to fall outside the scope of American children's literature since the original author, Helen Bannerman, was Scottish and lived in India at the time of the writing and the publication of *Little Black Sambo.* While considering Bannerman's original text and illustration in *Little Black Sambo,* my principal focus will be on the American illustrations of *Little Black Sambo* as it was published in the United States. *Little Black Sambo*'s American illustrators constructed childhood visually through their illustrations. The history of *The Story of Little Black Sambo* demonstrates how not only authors but also illustrators played a part in the visual representation of race in America.

---

[2] *Little Black Sambo* has undergone criticism in Japan as well. *Little Black Sambo* (the Japanese title is *Chibikuro Sambo*) was first published in Japan by Iwanami Shoten Publishing in 1953. The book was a pirated version of the 1927 Macmillan publication which contained drawings by Frank Dobias. Although there were over 40 other versions of *Sambo* published, the Iwanami version was the most popular, selling 1.2 million copies. However, as Bruce Wallace notes in the June 12, 2005 edition of the *Los Angeles Times*, a "mainly American campaign drove the book off Japanese shelves [in 1988]. [. . .] It [the selling of *Sambo*] sparked a bigger backlash in Washington, where there were accusations of entrenched racism against blacks among the Japanese and protests were held at the Japanese Embassy and threats made to boycott its cultural exports." In 1997, a race-free version of the book, *Chibikuro Sampo* ("sampo" means "taking a walk" in Japanese), was published by Kitaooji Shobo Publishing in Kyoto under the guidance of Mori Marimo, an educational psychologist at Shinshu University in Nagano. Wallace states, "Mori conducted academic experiments involving readers that he said showed the Japanese take nothing racist away from reading *Little Black Sambo.* He offered a group of kindergarteners and another of senior citizens a look at two versions of the story: one with the Dobias' drawings, another with the central character drawn as a black Labrador puppy. The test groups found both illustrated versions equally amusing. Ergo, no racism, Mori concluded." Bannerman's original was first published with a translation of Masahisa Nadamoto by Komichi Shobo Publishing, Tokyo, in 1999. The once-censored Iwanami version, with its controversial Dobias's illustrations and without the proper copyright, was re-released in April 2005 in Japan by a Tokyo based publisher Zuiunsya, because Iwanami's copyright expired after 50 years since its first appearance.

The Story of Little Black Sambo and Its Illustrations

Although originally a British children's book, *The Story of Little Black Sambo* has an intriguing American history reflecting views of race in America from its first American publication in 1900 through the latest version published in 2004. The argument which I put forward here is that the American illustrations of *The Story of Little Black Sambo* parallel historical attitudes towards African American people, showing the power of illustration in reflecting cultural attitudes and how African American childhood is constructed through visual means. While the various publications of *Uncle Tom's Cabin* since its original publication were adapted textually, the historical record of adaptation and re-adaptation of *The Story of Little Black Sambo* occurred visually through illustrations, marking the shifting societal relationship between races in the United States.

While debates about author Helen Bannerman and her text have been thoroughly discussed in literary and educational circles,[3] the American illustrations have received little critical attention. This lack of emphasis on the illustration is somewhat surprising as the American illustrations inform and reflect the time periods in which they were produced, demonstrating cultural attitudes concerning the construction of race in America. The illustrations that have accompanied the numerous publications of *The Story of Little Black Sambo* in the United States serve as a manifestation of American ideologies and white American perceptions concerning the levels of acceptance of African Americans. This unique literary record of the various versions of *Little Black Sambo* published since 1898 are here evaluated for the ways in which ideologies concerning race are portrayed and the reactions to such representations. The blame for *Sambo*'s historical controversy lies with the American illustrations, corresponding with white dominant majority attitudes towards African Americans, and demonstrating the power of illustration in culture in a time and place.

---

[3]Michelle Martin, *Brown Gold: Milestones of African American Children's Picture Books, 1845-2002.* (New York: Routledge, 2004); Bill Yoffee, *Black Sambo's Saga: The Story of Little Black Sambo Revisited at Age 98.* (Published Privately, 1997); Phyllis J.Yuill, *Little Black Sambo: A Closer Look: A History of Helen Bannerman's the Story of Little Black Sambo and Its Popularity/Controversy in the United States.* (New York: Racism and Sexism Resource Center for Educators, 1976).

Bannerman and the *Sambo* debates

A brief overview of Helen Bannerman's life shows her to be something other than the typical Victorian woman. Born as Brodie Cowan Watson in Edinburgh in 1862, Bannerman was the daughter of a Scottish minister. Bannerman spent most of her childhood abroad since her father's career as an army chaplain took him to various parts of the British Empire, including the island of Madeira. Located off the west coast of North Africa, Madeira's mixed population included peoples from Africa. Bannerman's exposure to various cultures acquainted her with a wider view of the world than most women of her time would have had, equipping her with life skills which enabled her to thrive in cultures of which she was not a native. In 1889, Bannerman married William Burney Bannerman, who was in the Indian Medical Service, and together they lived in India for the next 30 years. Helen Bannerman's life and actions in colonial India, as recounted by herself and her family and friends, showed her to be non-judgemental of differences in race and culture.

Yet Bannerman's first book for children has often been censored due to claims of racism. Bill Yoffee's study *Black Sambo's Saga: The Story of Little Black Sambo Revisited at Age 98* sums up such accusations by noting

> In recent years, the name *Black Sambo* has been the source of controversy. It has been associated with bigotry, racism, and prejudice. It has been considered a term of derision, the product of centuries of slavery, persecution and discrimination against African-Americans. It has been used as a stereotype for all of the alleged deficiencies of the race, and to this day many African-Americans take offence.[4]

Such accusations are often discussed by sympathetic critics, such as Julius Lester, who considers Bannerman to be a product of her times. Lester is one of the most widely awarded and respected African American authors today; his work *To Be A Slave* (1969) was one of the first reconstructed historical texts demonstrating alternative views of African American history through the use of slave narratives. Despite the criticism of *Little Black Sambo* which claims it to be a racist book, Lester defends the text but points out that we should "acknowledge the presence of unconscious bias in a literary text." In a similar tone of conciliation, Lester also added that "posterity has not been kind to Helen Bannerman." Today's authors of African American descent have various opinions about Bannerman resulting from their personal encounters with *The Story of Little Black Sambo*. Lester has recently rewritten Bannerman's text, changing the name to *Sam and the Tigers* (1996). When asked about his

---

[4]Yoffee, 3.

opinion of the book, Lester verbalized the duality of his feelings about *Little Black Sambo* and Bannerman:

> Is the book racist? In context, yes. *Little Black Sambo* was written [...] during this period that the leading universities engage in measuring the skulls of blacks and whites and Indians and on the basis of skull size and capacity determine the place of each on the evolutionary chain. *Little Black Sambo* appears during the time when racism is rampant and informs colonial and imperialistic policies of the U.S., German, French and English governments.

> Is *Little Black Sambo maliciously* racist? Not at all. It is a product of its times and as such, is rather benign. Bannerman does not use dialect and malapropisms. She does not deliberately or even consciously ridicule Little Black Sambo. In fact, there is a tension in the story between the illustrations and the story line. In the story line *Little Black Sambo* is quite a wonderful character.[5]

However, some critics found the caricatures of African Americans in *Little Black Sambo* and Bannerman's other works demeaning. In 1947 a critic asserted that "the original illustrations use all the usual stereotypes found in malicious cartoons of Negroes...the thick lips, the rolling eye, the bony knees, the fuzzy hair." In addressing the allegations that are made against Bannerman, one can only say that her intentions may never be truly known. However, Bannerman's children have commented that their mother would be saddened to know the accusations that have been made against her and her book.[6] Considering all the discussion and criticism about Bannerman, Lester concludes, "She was an educated woman. She was well aware of what she was doing in placing a black boy in India. She was creating fantasy. The story has always been a fantasy, which should be obvious since tigers do not talk to little boys and ask for their clothes."[7]

Today, much like Harriet Beecher Stowe's *Uncle Tom's Cabin*, *The Story of Little Black Sambo* is known *about* but not actually read. Sambo holds a place in the minds of most Americans as being a racist book, but in my teaching experience of reading *Little Black Sambo* to university students in such diverse places as Mississippi, San Diego, and the United Kingdom, only a small handful of university students have read the story. Even fewer know the publication story behind the book. Bannerman's story and illustrations were not originally

---

[5]Julius Lester, "Little Black Sambo by Bannerman: Thoughts on Racism in Children's Literature." CHILDLIT listserv, 1995. Conversations about *Little Black Sambo*.
[6]Elizabeth Hay, *Sambo Sahib: The Story of Helen Bannerman Author of' Little Black Sambo* (Edinburgh: Paul Harris Publishing, 1981), 155.
[7]Ibid.

written for publication; *Sambo* was written for Bannerman's two young daughters.

Publishing History and Early Responses

Today, copyright is strongly protected by law. Over one hundred years ago, the publishing world was different. So when Mrs. Alice M. E. Bond, a family friend also living in India, read the book at the Bannerman's home and asked to serve as Bannerman's literary agent since she was travelling to London, Bannerman had requested that Bond not sell the copyright. Grant Richards was the first publisher interested in *The Story of Little Black Sambo*. After viewing the book, Richards immediately offered to publish the book under the condition that he owned the copyright. He offered £5—equivalent to approximately £1,787 in today's value. The time it took for correspondence to travel worked in favour of Richards, and two days after Richard's offer, Mrs. Bond agreed to the sale of the copyright.[8] Almost immediately, disagreements between Bannerman and the publisher occurred, but with no copyright to secure her opinions on the details of publication, Bannerman was powerless to stop Richards from publishing *Little Black Sambo* however he pleased. Richard's publication was quickly printed in order to make *Little Black Sambo* available to Christmas shoppers.

Although *Little Black Sambo* was quickly rushed to publication and disagreements existed between the author and publisher, *Sambo* was an immediate success. *Sambo* was also not a children's story that was quickly to be forgotten, as is proved by its longevity in the publishing world. *Little Black Sambo* was initially regarded as a book that positively portrayed Black characters, especially in comparison to the more negative books of the time that depicted blacks as simple and uncivilized. Critics agreed that Sambo was something new and special. Immediate reviews highly praised Bannerman's work, and the book sold well. While today's university age students are unfamiliar with *Little Black Sambo* due to wide spread banning of the book which began in the 1960s, older generations either know the story or know of the story.

Twenty-one thousand copies were in print only a year after its initial publication.[9] Its publication date, 31st Oct 1899, and its inexpensive pricing at one shilling and six pence (approximately £1.32 today), made it a perfect Christmas gift, which was exactly what Richards had intended. An early review of nursery books appeared in *The Spectator* on 2 December 1899. Criticizing

---

[8]Hay, 17.
[9]Yoffee, 4.

most of the ten books it reviewed for being too didactic and parent centred, the review continued:

> Very different must be the verdict on that most attractive little book *The Story of Little Black Sambo.* It has been briefly noticed in these columns before, but no comparison between old and new fashioned nursery books would be quite fair without allowing Little Black Sambo to give his protest in favour of recent books. His history was not written with one eye on parents and guardians, or the inconsistency of mixing up the African type of black with delightful adventures with tigers in an Indian jungle would never have been allowed to pass. As it is, Little Black Sambo makes his simple and direct appeal in the greatest realm of make-believe without paying the slightest attention to the unities or caring in the least about anything but the amusement of the little boys and girls for whom he was obviously created. Every parent should at once get the book and give it both to the nursery and the schoolroom. It is impossible to deny that among this year's Christmas books *Little Black Sambo* is, to use his own classic phrase, far and away 'the grandest tiger in the jungle.'[10]

Ironically, this review praises aspects of *Little Black Sambo* that later critics identify as faults. Clearly, at the time of its British publication, *The Story of Little Black Sambo* was understood in the manner in which Bannerman first wrote it; it is an adventure story in a make-believe land where the main character, who happens to be Black, is successfully heroic because of his intelligence, not his colour.

Besides presenting a black hero, *The Story of Little Black Sambo* was the first book of its kind in children's literature in other ways. Elizabeth Hay points out in her critical biography of Helen Bannerman, *Sambo Sahib: The Story of Little Black Sambo and Helen Bannerman,* that

> *Little Black Sambo* embodied nearly all the principles on which present-day books for young children are based and was revolutionary in its day. [...] The pictures were direct and vivid, and printed in primary colours. [...] [It] is action-packed and yet repetitive. It also lacked what had been considered essential in a children's book up to that moment: a moral purpose or improving tone.[11]

Printed two years before Beatrix Potter's *Peter Rabbit,*[12] the size of Bannerman's book was small enough for a young child to hold in their hands. Critics have praised the book as entertaining and humorous; Elizabeth Gard commented

---

[10]Quoted in Hay, 28.
[11]Hay, 1.
[12]Privately printed first and then by Richards as part of The Dumpy Book series of which *The Story of Little Black Sambo* was a part of.

[I]t's not difficult to see why *Little Black Sambo* has always been the favourite. [...] Each picture exactly illustrates a moment in the story [...]. The simple words, and the highly effective repetition [...] rivet the attention of both reader and listener. Mrs. Bannerman seems to have fallen completely instinctively into just the right style for children.[13]

While the size, shape, and content were child-centred, *Little Black Sambo* also contained a fantasy element that children loved, and yet this fantasy aspect of the story is most often forgotten today.

Today's reviews of Sambo are less flattering. Although the story has been in constant publication since 1899, *The Story of Little Black Sambo* seems to be unable to overcome its own tragic history. Critic Phyllis Yuill notes that controversies surrounding the book began appearing in professional journals in the mid-1940s and are maintained to this day. Critics, parents, librarians, and authors still consider this divisive book a classic work in children's literature, much loved and fondly remembered by more than one generation of Americans. In 1971, Selma Lanes noted, "In loving Sambo, unreservedly, in some way, every white had the feeling that he was also accepting the black man as a fellow human being. The nursery bookshelf was integrated, and no prejudice could exist in a home where *Little Black Sambo* and *Peter Rabbit* stood side by side on the same shelf."[14]

Michelle Martin reiterates Lanes' discussion when she states "other critics felt that while many white Americans early in the twentieth century considered black people invisible within the culture, Sambo made whites acknowledge the humanity in black people,"[15] an aspect somewhat forgotten due to the popularity of minstrels and other literary works that only provided a view of the black American as comical. Others believe its historical value to be more important, citing that it should be housed in collections as a remembrance of racial children's literature.

In spite of its continuous print record and historical and literary value, much criticism is levelled against *The Story of Little Black Sambo*. While these concerns about setting, theme, and character names are discussed in most criticisms of the book, the most damning—and most relevant to this thesis— element is the illustrations that reveal a history of their own. Since neither Bannerman nor Richards retained the copyright, the story often appeared with

---

[13]Nickolas Tucker, *Suitable for Children: Controversies in Children's Literature* (London: Sussex University Press; Chatto & Windus, 1976), 78.
[14]Quoted in Yuill, 9.
[15]Michelle Martin, "Hey, Who's the Kid with the Green Umbrella?": Re-Evaluating the Black-a-Moor and Little Black Sambo," *The Lion and the Unicorn* 22, no.2 (1998), 147-62.

illustrations other than the author's own. Such illustrations are often pictures that are stereotypical in their portrayal of Blacks in jungle or plantation settings. Racist ideology against African Americans in the United States is witnessed through the illustrations of *Little Black Sambo*. When viewed today, such a historical record of illustrations serves to recall the painful history of African Americans in the United States.

Changing Illustrations / Changing Ideologies

The historical record of the adaptations and re-adaptations of *Little Black Sambo* begins with the original creator, Helen Bannerman. While Bannerman's intent in publishing *Little Black Sambo* is debated, her artistic style should also be evaluated. Bannerman showed little consistency as artist in her original illustration of *The Story of Little Black Sambo* (1898). Cartoonish in overall style, the six different views of Sambo offered by Bannerman reveal six different looking Sambos.[16] Helen Bannerman herself claimed that her artistic renderings were less than perfect, asking that a family friend never be shown the painting Bannerman made of her so as not to cause offence. The books by Bannerman that were published after *The Story of Little Black Sambo* maintained her cartoonish style no matter the race of the main character.[17] But when publishers chose their own illustrations for *Little Black Sambo,* the differences in ideology and perception of the book changed drastically.

In 1900, *Sambo*'s British publisher Grant Richards sold the American copyright to Fredrick A. Stokes of New York, and the first authorized version of *Little Black Sambo* was published in the United States in the same form as the Richards' version but with a different cover.[18] Only five years later, other publishers began to make their own "unauthorized" versions of this book. In 1905, Reilly and Britton of Chicago included *The Story of Little Black Sambo* in their Christmas Stocking Series, along with *The Night before Christmas, Cinderella and the Sleeping Beauty, A Child's Visit to the Zoo, Fairy Tales from Andersen,* and *Fairy Tales from Grimm.* This was the first of many versions with either doctored adaptations of Bannerman's illustrations or with altogether

---

[16]Yoffee, 7.

[17]An exception was her last book, *Little White Squibba,* published in 1966 posthumously. This unfinished manuscript was found in Bannerman's papers after her death and was completed by her daughter, Day. Its style of illustration is completely different, showing Bannerman's growth as an artist, but also Day's influence on the final product.

[18]Bannerman objected to the cover Grant Richards chose for the first publication in 1899. Ironically, the cover for the Stokes publication in the United States was changed to Bannerman's illustration of Sambo, even though it was a publication into which she had no input.

new illustrations. From 1917 throughout 1950, versions of Bannerman's *Little Black Sambo* were published almost every year.[19]

In the 1908 version of *The Story of Little Black Sambo*, Reilly and Briton included new illustrations by John R. Neill, who would soon after be famous for his *Oz* illustrations. Whereas Bannerman was a less talented illustrator with a caricature style of illustration, Neill's illustrations clearly show an influence of the minstrel tradition, dehumanizing Sambo. American publishers in general did not retain Bannerman's illustrations. A possible explanation for this might include the fact that Bannerman's illustrations contained aspects of the story that the publishers did not embrace. The setting of post-Bannerman versions of *The Story of Little Black Sambo* has always been debated. Bannerman loosely refers to "the Jungle" in her text but never identifies a specific setting, understanding that Bannerman's fantasyland was her setting.

Bannerman's illustrations are also vague, giving very little background illustration. In Bannerman's mind, the land where Sambo lives exists only in the world of imagination. But in American illustrators minds—and thus reflected in their illustrations—Sambo has lived in Africa or in the southern United States. According to the illustrations that accompanied the written texts, Sambo did not live in India until the 1930s. These specific settings encumbered the story, implying political stances or ideologies unrelated to Bannerman's original fantasy.

Along with changes in setting, American publishers and illustrators also change the visual image of the characters. John Neill's 1908 version as published by The Reilly & Briton Co. is one of the earliest and most shocking publications of *Little Black Sambo*, which borrows Bannerman's original text. The grotesque features given to Sambo and his family emphasize the Social Darwinist view of a hierarchy of races representing the evolution of humanity along the lines of Darwin's evolution of species. Sambo is illustrated as a monkey. In comparing Neill's illustration of a monkey in the Oz series to his illustration of Sambo, his views—that blacks are the missing evolutionary link and are more closely related to monkeys rather than whites—are clearly evident.

Another famous American illustrator, John Gruelle, illustrated *All About Sambo* in 1917. Gruelle, who is best known for his books about *Raggedy Ann Stories* (1918), illustrated the jungle background and provided a "noble savage" in a loincloth. Gruelle included additional animals that, like Sambo, watched the tigers as they fought amongst themselves to decide who was the "grandest Tiger

---

[19]Not only were illustrations changed, but the Sambo text was also changed. One author, Frank ver Beck, managed to create a new line of Sambo stories in the late 1920s and throughout the 1930s. He created such titles as *Little Black Sambo and the Baby Elephant, Sambo and the Tiger Kittens, Sambo in the Bear's Den (1930)*, and *Little Black Sambo and the Monkey People (1935)*.

in the Jungle." Sambo in his 'natural' unclothed state appears at peace with the other animals in the jungle, much like fairy tales in which the pure innocent child is at one with nature. The tigers seemingly depict civilisation, since Gruelle positioned them as sitting in a meeting with paws waving in humanistic form, deciding who is the grandest tiger in the jungle. When a civilized decision cannot be agreed upon, fighting commences in an attempt to settle the dispute through physical domination. The reader views Sambo as he watches from a safe distance, choosing not to be involved in such matters that are physically beyond him. The monkey shares this gaze, reinforcing the Sambo/monkey connection.

More confusion over setting was apparent in versions printed in 1918 and 1919. Florence White Williams' illustrations place Sambo in the southern United States rather than Bannerman's make believe country, while M. A. Donohue & Company's publication (author/illustrator not credited) in 1919 has Sambo's father dressed in traditional African clothing with Sambo dressed as a plantation slave with his wide straw hat. Sambo's father provides him the clothing of slavery, a statement recalling that warring tribes in Africa sold fellow Africans who were prisoners of war to the slave traders. Other editions from the same era show Sambo first in a grass skirt and then in southern American clothing, constructing a clothed state as equal with civilisation while the natural state is that of the savage. The philosophical justification for slavery as a civilizing process that enhanced the African race is reinforced.

It was during this time that race riots were occurring in the larger cities of the United States. The summer of 1919 was known as the "Red Summer" due to the number of deaths in race riots. Richard Wormser writes, "The Chicago riot was part of a national racial frenzy of clashes, massacres, and lynchings throughout the North and the South. All of the incidents were initiated by whites."[20] While hundreds of citizens were injured or killed in the summer of 1919, US illustrators were depicting African Americans as uncivilised savages.

Throughout publications in the 1920s, clothing continued to be utilised as a symbol of civilisation. Sambo was illustrated as a savage native who became civilised through "dressing right"—which meant dressing white. The myths and stereotypes, which depict African Americans as savage, native, and only civilised through their contact with the white population, are reinforced for a new generation. Sambo's fear is evident as he runs from the jungle partially naked, disempowering Bannerman's original strong courageous character. Sambo's clothed/naked/clothed circumstances are emphasised over the plot in which Sambo shows his intelligence by defeating the tigers.

---

[20]Richard Wormser, *The Rise and Fall of Jim Crow* (New York: St. Martin's Press, 2003).

The minstrel tradition reappeared in such publications as Albert Whitman & Co., 1926 publication, illustrated by Cobb X. Shinn. This edition, which was also republished in 1935, uses Bannerman's "poses" or positioning of character, but paints them in the minstrel tradition, blackface with large eyes and mouth. Sambo is once again constructed in this illustration as a savage native of Africa. In Macmillian's publication in 1927, illustrator Frank Dobias completes the savage Sambo image, providing him with a club and tiger skin outfit. In comparing Bannerman's original illustration with those done in the 1920s, Bannerman's illustrations at the time of Sambo's first publications seem coarse. However, compared to these later images, Bannerman's illustrations are far less culpable of racist intent than the minstrel images which were still in existence in the 1920s.

In more ways than one, colour was an issue in the publication of the Sambo books. Almost all of the Sambo books were printed in full colour, including Bannerman's original. However, in the books of limited colour (basic three tones) or partial colour, in which some pictures were in black and white, it is interesting also to note the difference in how Sambo is illustrated. Sambo in black and white becomes almost demon like, with the white reflection on his head taking on the appearance of horns. Illustrators seemed to struggle with how to realistically portray someone with dark skin. While other media allowed illustrators to work in shades, black and white illustrators seemed to struggle with the concept of using lighter greys to take the place of browns in portraying the hero. Sambo was and only could ever be all black.

To further reinforce evolutionary ideas of the relationship between Africans (no matter their location) and apes, a monkey began to appear as an additional character. Charles E. Graham & Company's version included a monkey in the bottom right hand corner who is laughing and pointing at Sambo as he cries, an open invitation for the reader to also laugh at Sambo.

The "coloured" Sambo in the very same book has a very different look. In illustrating the same character in such different ways, the illustrator creates ambiguity which the reader is to feel for Sambo. This ambiguity was faced by African Americans in reality as well as viewed in literature. Moreover, these depictions reinforced the view that Sambo's blackness made him a laughable character, unheroic and animalistic.

While publishers contrasted the views of Sambo in colour and in black and white, school readers which included *Little Black Sambo* also showed the differences in races through illustration. Sambo's appearance is wild, uncivilized, and raw, while the white children are illustrated realistically in the same book, resulting in a construction of African American childhood as something different and foreign to white childhood.

Some illustrators attempted to make Sambo into a book for very young readers, offering a romanticized black character that white readers could safely embrace due to his cuteness, making him a pet instead of a person. This is especially evident in Samuel Gabriel Sons publication in 1921 in which Sambo is closer to an elf in appearance. Sambo with his monkey sidekick appears even in these readers for the youngest of children, supporting stereotypes as previously noted. This monkey mimics Sambo's actions, just as it was thought that the African American man needed to mimic the humanity of the white man.

However, in 1931 the representations of Sambo began to transform. Although Yuill notes that the criticism against Bannerman's book did not begin till the 1940s, publishers were already responding to movements in the market. Fern Bisel Peat illustrated *Little Black Sambo* reflecting an Indian culture. Sambo has earrings and a slant to his eyes previously unseen, reflecting an Asian if not Indian influence. This morphing of Sambo into an Indian location continues today and reflects the continuing confusion over Bannerman's setting, disregarding her fantasy land setting for the country she lived in at the time of writing, India. These new illustrations show sensitivity towards culture not seen in earlier publications. However, it is an Indian culture that is presented, not an African/African American culture.

That is not to say that suddenly white America had seen the error of its ways and would no longer tolerate the degrading images previously printed in connection with the *Little Black Sambo* story. In 1931, McLoughlin Brothers published Hildegard Luprian's illustrations that identify Sambo as a pickaninny; again, the influence of the minstrel tradition is apparent.

Fern Bisel Peat again illustrated Sambo in 1932 in the Calico Classic series. While the illustration style was set within the context of the series, i.e. the idea of the series was to illustrate them as cloth dolls, Sambo is reminiscent of the Scarecrow from John R. Neill's *Wizard of Oz* illustrations. Comparing the three images, the confusion in presentation is plain to see. Sambo is Asian/Indian, minstrel pickaninny, and a scarecrow rag doll. None of these illustrations represent Sambo in a positive light. Peat's Asian/Indian Sambo is erotically othered in an Eastern setting and in body positioning. Luprian's illustrations offer the audience an object to laugh at and mock since the goal is to laugh at Sambo's fear. Peat's cloth doll suggests memories of the Scarecrow from *The Wizard of Oz* who is not only weak, but also searching for a brain. All three illustrations invite the gaze of the audience, objectifying Sambo as black, different than white, and therefore other.

Since the 1930s, Sambo has had a confused ethnic background. Illustrators and publishers have constructed him as Indian, while others attempted to return Sambo to his black roots, although Sambo's facial features make him look like a white child with a darker complexion. Once the Indian-ness (and otherness) of

Sambo had become established, *Little Black Sambo* became a "safe" book to publish. Even though he was still called Little Black Sambo, Sambo became white in 1967 for a claymation book with his parents very Indian in their style of dress. And as early as 1949, Sambo completely lost his blackness in various versions of *Little Brave Sambo*. His Indian-ness and his blackness are both erased as Sambo became a Native American Indian/white child in book and record in 1949, 1950, circa 1960, and 1971.

The debates about Sambo are refreshed with every new publication of *Little Black Sambo*. Three new versions of Sambo have received critical acclaim while simultaneously being condemned by others. Fred Marcellino's *The Story of Little Babaji* shows his interpretation of Bannerman's work in the Indian theme. Julius Lester and Jerry Pinkney, both of African American descent, place the story in a fantasyland, just as Bannerman wanted, in their rewritten version called *Sam and the Tigers* (1996). Lester has been vocal about his mixed feelings of Bannerman's original work. Louise Kennedy, in her article for *The Boston Globe* entitled "New Storybook Reopen Old Wounds," quotes Lester: "Very unconsciously, with no malice aforethought, Bannerman was reflecting her times. And the fact that she was hurting black people never entered her mind. Which doesn't let her off the hook." The article continues, "Lester acknowledges the power of Bannerman's story, in which a boy, pursued by tigers, appeases them with his fine new clothes; he watches as the angry tigers spin into butter, which his mother uses for pancakes. 'This is a wonderful story,' Lester says, but one that has caused a lot of pain." Continuing to explain his feelings about Bannerman, Lester commented:

> We, blacks and whites, can acknowledge that the names of the characters and Bannerman's illustrations demean blacks. This is not because Bannerman was a rabid racist but because of the times in which the book was published and subsequent historical associations. Acknowledging the racism in *Little Black Sambo* does not mean one must deny one's love for the book.[21]

Christopher Bing is one author who unashamedly loves *Little Black Sambo*. His version published in 2001 uses Bannerman's original text, a choice that has brought *Little Black Sambo* into debate. For Bing, this project is an attempt to rehabilitate a misunderstood artefact. "I would like to dispel the cloud around it," he says. "I don't ever want a black child to pick up the book and look at the images and feel insulted . . . I want a child to feel just the wonder I did as a child." For Christopher Bing, the text he chose to illustrate is "the perfect story." "It's got everything," Bing says. "An exotic hero, an exotic location. It's got

---

[21]Louise Kennedy, "New Storybook Reopens Old Wounds," *The Boston Globe,* 14 December 2003.

danger—the tigers—and then he outwits them. And for a kid in America, the best thing of all: It had pancakes coming out the ears."[22] This story also has, as Bing acknowledges, a deeply troubled history that starts right at the title. Bing's illustrations are very different to the images seen in Bannerman's original version or in the grotesque examples from the early twentieth century. His attempt to realistically portray a fantasyland is commendable, but some critics are still unable to put Sambo's past in the past.

A vivid example of Sambo's illustrated and turbulent history is contained in three versions of the same reader, *My Book House*. In the 1937 edition, the story titled *Little Black Sambo* retains Bannerman's original text, but her illustrations are replaced with doctored, minstrel-influenced illustrations. In the 1965 version, the original text remains with an added subtitle, *A Tale of India*. The illustrations reflect the title and display an Indian setting with all characters in Indian style clothing, including Black Jumbo in a turban. By the 1971 version, the illustrations remain the same, but the story is no longer *Little Black Sambo*. It is now titled *Rama and the Tigers: A Tale of India*. Sambo's positive reception in 1899—with negative criticism starting in the early 1900s—and shifting identity from the 1930s onward reflect an unsettled American approach to racial difference in the United States.

It is this troubling history of Sambo's past that is extended into other children's books in the 1930s. From 1930 through 1939, *Little Black Sambo* was published nineteen times, one edition almost every six months over a ten-year span. The changes through illustration reflect an interesting ideological evolution of acceptance of African Americans into mainstream dominant—but no longer solely white—society. Through Sambo's publication history in the United States, one can trace the shifting constructions of African American childhood through illustration. As authors and illustrators faced the 1930s, existing constructs could be either maintained and defended or changed and celebrated. The literary foundations were set for constructing and re-constructing African American childhood in the 1930s.

---

[22]Ibid.

CHAPTER TWO

PICTURE BOOK AS CONCEPTUAL SPACE: SPATIAL TRANSFORMATION IN TOVE JANSSON'S *BOOK ABOUT MOOMIN, MYMBLE AND LITTLE MY*

ELINA DRUKER

[*Editor's note*: The material in this article was originally presented at the 31st annual conference of the Children's Literature Association at California State University, Fresno, in 2004.]

The Finland-Swedish artist, novelist, and children's book author Tove Jansson was born in 1914 and grew up as part of the Swedish-speaking minority in Finland. Jansson began her Moomin series in 1945. Her first picture book, *The Book about Moomin, Mymble and Little My,* was published in 1952.[23] It expresses a radical new way of thinking and indicates a break with earlier narrative principles in Finnish as well as in Nordic picture book aesthetics.

The Book about Moomin, Mymble and Little My starts in a dark forest. Moomintroll is on his way home from the milk-shop, carrying a milk bucket. During his journey Moomin is subjected to various trials and encounters both helpers and adversaries. He meets Mymble and joins her in her search for her missing little sister My. What the story is about seems however to be of secondary importance to *how* it is told. The game of searching that is initiated in the first scene, and the play with various surfaces and layers, perforations, and missing segments suggest the picture book as a site of adventure, theatrical play, and fantasy, where the role of the reader is activated.

Spatial innovation is a prominent feature in this picture book. Holes in different sizes and shapes perforate the pages, revealing parts of the next spread and framing and focusing on specific details. The perforations function as visual

---

[23]Tove Jansson, *Hur gick det sen? Boken om Mumin, och lilla My*, trans. *The Book about Moomin, Mymble and Little My* (London: Ernest Benn, 1953).

page turners but also as doorways that lead us further into the story. Through the perforations we get clues and suggestions of what might happen in the coming scene. There is a preoccupation with movement from page to page, through openings and gaps, where the letters correspond to the illustrations and seem to move with the pictures. The sequential rhythm of the linear, literary time is occasionally twisted.

The spatial-temporal construction of a picture book consists of a literary element—words—and a visual element—a sequence of pictures. It is the combination of words and images in their capacity to express both temporal and spatial qualities that creates an illusion of movement and spatiality. A spatial-temporal quality is furthermore implied through the material form of the picture book, for example through the act of turning of the pages.[24] In *The Book about Moomin, Mymble and Little My,* the relationship between words and pictures is dynamic. Even the letters are used to create a sense of movement, to express volume and size. The fonts simulate handwritten text with flowing, cursive, or joined-up slanted letters. When Little My speaks, the print is diminished to illustrate her tiny physical size. When Moomintroll takes a leap, the words leap as well. The sentence "They hunted low, they hunted high" is bent to mirror the motion of climbing on giant boulders in a nightmarish cave.[25] Both the letters and the sentences they form are used to create images on the page. The visual form of the text is thus spatialised. A rhythm and a structure is also created through a repetition of the sentence "what do you think happened then?" that concludes each scene.

Moomintroll from the milk-shop ran with milk for Mother in his can,
up through the forest dark and wide, wind in the tall trees moaned and sighed.
The road was eerie, long and drear, 'twas six o'clock and dusk was near.
How tired he was feeling—when—what do you think happened then?

The terror of the dark woods in the opening scene is soon transformed to light. However, no ordinary daylight illuminates this strange landscape. The colours, yellow and purple, orange, black, and blue, are artificial and combined in an alarming fashion.[26] The one colour missing is green, the colour

---

[24]Johanna Drucker proposes that the act of turning pages is a convention that is "inherently visual as well as temporal and spatial" in *The Century of Artists'Books* (New York: Granary Books, 1995), 175. Drucker does not include picture books in her study of the artists' books, but her study is relevant in a discussion of the material aspects of the book medium,
[25]I am using the first English translation from 1953.
[26]For a more detailed discussion concerning the function of colours, see Boel Westin, "Bilderbokens estetik. Tove Jansson som bilderbokskonstnär" in *Svensklärarföreningens årsskrift* (1983), 70-73.

representing nature, summer, the colouring of natural world. The drastic colours and the striking illumination of the landscape, described in the text and further accentuated in the illustrations, are used to create a strange and nightmarish journey. A central theme of Tove Jansson's Moomin World, throughout her entire production, is a tension between the idyllic and the chaotic.[27] The main characters are transported through a series of extraordinary scenes. Recognizable everyday objects as vacuum cleaners or milk buckets meet the fantastic and abstract. By using an archetypical and mythical narrative pattern and changing its form, altering the appearance of the narration, as well as using irony and antithesis, a sense of ambiguity is established. Tove Jansson has explained that the first Moomin books were initiated by the war as an imaginary escape from the harsh wartime reality. The complexity of the form and the changing mode of spatial and temporal relations express a strong feeling of disorder. The setting is drastically changed on every opening without a logical connection concerning the landscape. This kind of shifting visual experiences of the landscape and of space as such can be compared to the worlds created by Lewis Carroll in the books about Alice, where the changes of the environment express the underlying theme of searching and identity.

The disposition of the images in this picture book consists of flat surfaces of colour and voids. The visual space between the entrance on the left side and the exit on the right side, between the foreground and distance, creates a dynamic perspective that is at once clear and confusing. The distinct colours and the geometrical forms, combined with treacherous spaces and dramatic events that seem to await as soon as we turn the page, create a sense of uncertainty. We might find the scenes amusing and comical or thoroughly frightening. In either case, the sensation arises not only from the actions taking place, but from the process of creative exploration of the narrative space.

The opening scene indicates that a certain kind of attitude is required in the reading act. Fiction signals its own fictionality. These rules are, in fact, set on the book cover. The key to how to read the book is presented already outside the fictional sphere, before the narration begins, as we see the main characters of the book peeking out through a round cut-out window on the cover. The changing conception of the child and the implied child reader is reflected in the choice and forming of the narrative subject as well as in the way reality and fiction are

---

[27] Boel Westin discusses the tension between the ordered and the chaotic of the Moomin World in her dissertation, *Familjen i dalen: Tove Janssons muminvärld* (Stockholm: Bonnier, 1988). See also Westin, "Konsten som äventyr. Tove Jansson och bilderboken" in *Vår moderna bilderbok* (Stockholm: Raben&Sjögren, 1991), 58. Also Riikka Stewen stresses the underlying structure of conflict in her article "Kuinkas sitten kävikään? Ja katsomisen aika" in *Avoin ja suljettu. Kirjoituksia 1950-luvusta suomalaisessa kulttuurissa*, (Helsinki: Suomalaisen kirjallisuuden seura, 1992), 20-29.

presented. Generally, one can say that the Finnish post-war picture book is a text-driven narrative where text is dominant in relationship to the illustrations. In the case of *The Book about Moomin, Mymble and Little My*, the combination of words and images is dynamic and complex. The picture book as a physical object—with its material qualities such as its covers, turning of pages, or perforations—is used in the text-image narration, resulting in a picture book that is complex and offers many levels of reading. Even if there are clear tendencies toward a more integrated text-image relationship in the Finnish picture book during this time period, Jansson stands out as a unique picture book artist and is undoubtedly ahead of her time.

A central theme in this picture book is reality versus imagination. Playing with and questioning the fictional illusion draws attention to the means and conventions of communication. A game with different worlds and layers of fictionality is established, as mentioned above, on the book cover. The covers literally function as external boundaries of the book, confining and separating fiction from reality. As we open the book, a person who seems to be the publisher appears on the endpaper. He is holding a large pair of scissors in his hands and is proudly presenting the actual hole above his head, with the text "The holes are cut at Schildts" above it, naming the publishing house and thus foregrounding the aspect of the mechanical production of a book. At the same time he seems to be announcing the beginning of the show, gesturing elegantly towards the other half of the double spread where the main characters Moomin, Mymble and Little My are posing, turned towards us, as if pictured on a poster. The story has not started yet, but the main characters (as well as the milk bucket) are introduced here. Step by step, the reader is drawn into the fictional sphere.

The use of the materiality of the picture book in this manner signals that the characters are in fact fictional characters inside a fictional world, in a book, consisting of white sheets of paper and lines and surfaces of colour. The setting is neither a geographical landscape nor a traditional fairy tale world. The picture book medium has a clearly sequential and continuous structure, but in this case, each opening also functions as a separate space, yet connected to the whole. The perforations stimulate imaginative activity and create a tension, a rhythm and a dynamic motion forward. They suggest that something might happen, something is implied, but not yet visible. Gaps in the paper, the empty space itself, includes the notion of potential, a promise but also a thrill, an uncertainty since we do not know quite what to expect.

The technique with perforated pages is not merely a narrative technique, but functions also as a spatialisation technique. The temporal succession created between the two openings is never a straight line, even if the ongoing movement is clearly chronological and occurs from left to right. What happens when the spatial and the temporal fields are opened in two directions? In the scene where Moomintroll and Mymble crawl through a jar and meet the terrifying Gaffsie, the entrances and exits are accentuated through the character's body language. Our gaze is drawn towards the opening of the cave, situated on the right page, behind Gaffsie. In the cave—formed as and framed by a perforation—we get a glimpse of Mymble with a horrified expression and nervous body gesture. She is visualized twice on this double-spread, both on the left page, confronting Gaffsie, and on the right page as we get a glimpse of her inside the cave. The temporal order is clear, the picture is read from left to right, and the scene in the cave takes place after the confrontation with Gaffsie. At the same time this small image functions as a premonition, an implication of something alarming that will take place. The linear temporality and order of the narration suddenly take a bounce forward. These gaps, framing parts of an image, work in two temporal directions. The linear and sequential continuity becomes disconnected for a short while, and yet continues as we turn the next page.

A similar kind of play with different levels of the image is used on the previous opening. We see a placard presenting a picture of Little My, announcing that she is missing. The exact same image of My is used in the next scene, as we see her standing behind the jar that Mymble and Moomin just crawled through. The first image is a sign that signifies and depicts Little My. In the next scene, framed by a round opening, the actual My is presented. The scene is interesting concerning the level of the image. There is a clear difference between the image of Little My on the placard and the image of the actual Little My in the later scene. Like any frame, the gap defines and outlines that which is enclosed. We can see what shall happen next in the story, but also backwards as the gaps allow us to see a glance of the previous page. In this case with the two different images of My, it also transforms the impression. The relationship between the two images of little My indicates a transformation of the level of an image. In the first scene, the image of My is depicted as a separate entity, framed and pictorialised. In the following scene the same image, although differently framed, seems to be a part of narration. These two levels of image offer two different methods of representation.

The hole pierces the page between two spatial entities, connecting the two areas, but also transforming them during the act of turning the pages. In these empty spaces new stories are created. As the main characters accidentally frighten a sleeping fillyjonk, she actually escapes through the page and "leaps to the next page of this book." A hole is ripped in the fabric of the drawing. A picture within a picture is created. After she has been frightened by Moomin and his friends on the left page, we see her from a distance on the right page, framed by the torn paper. We see a frightened woman who is running away over the hills in a highly dramatic fashion, silhouetted against the stormy sky. This romantic scene functions as a quotation, as an allusion to other stories and genres. It is a story within a story. For the first time a hole is pictured with proposed three-dimensionality, and the edges of the hole, drawn with precision, influences and articulates the emptiness that it surrounds. The line functions as a contour of the form rather than as an outline; nuances of line quality define and point out the assumed three-dimensional volume rather than simply marking the edge of a two-dimensional shape. The gap has plastic qualities. The torn page doesn't merely represent a torn page, it *is* a torn page.

> The fillyjonk, with frightened look,
> leaped to the next page of this book.
> Just see the hole that she has made,
> A very large one, I'm afraid,
> But after her we'll go again.
> What do you think happened then?

The narrator steps forward in the text. She points out the fact that the scared fillyjonk actually pierces the page by diving through it. She also calls attention to the fact that the story is taking place in a book, underlying its fictional status. With small letters, placed under a white, square space, the narrator urges the reader to draw a picture of fillyjonk: "The fillyjonk when she has calmed herself—try and draw her for yourself," offering an empty area for this purpose and signing her signature in the lower corner of the message. Suddenly, the narrator steps forward by occupying a space. The difference between the image field where the actions take place and this surface, occupied by the narrator's message, is significant. The signature "Tove" in the lower right corner of the letter is worthy a note. This kind of self-reflexivity brings a mechanism of paradox into play. The text is embedded in the image. It is made visual, and yet is following literary conventions. As Victor Stoichita demonstrates in his study of the painting as a "self-aware image," art work with self-reflective qualities often thematises the status and boundaries of the painting.[28] In this scene, the signature has qualities that are outside the image. The commentary and the signature are outside the primary text and image.

There is another element in this image that foregrounds the play with the limits of the two-dimensional picture and the concept of the page. The scene is carefully observed by a tiny character placed in the margin. He is standing

---

[28]See Victor Stoichita's study *The Self-Aware Image. An Insight into Early Modern Meta-Painting,* trans. Anne-Marie Glasheen (Cambridge: Cambridge Univ. Press, 1997). Arguing that panel painting, from its origins in the Early Renaissance, was a "self-aware image," Stoichita shows that art and its boundaries were frequently thematised. Concerning contextual self-projection in form of inscriptions and signatures, see chapter eight of this text.

above the piece of paper. The scene makes no sense as a representation of physical space, the creature is standing *in* the background surface rather than in front of it. The main plot and the subsidiary ones take place in the same spatial space, and yet their relationship is inconsistent, even contradictory. The text establishes a connection between the two levels of narration. There is, however, nothing that indicates that the main characters are even aware of the subsidiary events. The characters seem to, however, be able to transform the composition of the image field itself.

The use of a blank sheet of paper resembles a scene in Lawrence Sterne's classic metafictional novel, *The Life and Opinions of Tristram Shandy, Gentleman* (1759-1767). Here an empty page is left for the reader, allowing him to create his own picture of the beautiful Widow Wadman, who is so beautiful that it is, according to the narrator, impossible to describe her beauty in words.[29] As in Sterne's work, this kind of self-reflexive commentary calls attention to the materiality of the text. Patricia Waugh discusses fictional writing which self-consciously and systematically draws attention to its status as an artefact in order to pose questions about the relationship between fiction and reality. Waugh points out that in providing a critique of their own methods of construction, metafictional texts not only examine the basic structures of narrative fiction, but they also explore the possible fictionality of the world outside the literary fictional text.[30] Metafictional use of images, framing as well as the representation of a "picture in a picture" can be considered as a practice focusing on a meta-artistic discourse. Self-reflective focus on the picture book medium brings to play the elements of the page, the margins and the frames, or, as in the case of the blank space, the emptiness of the surface. In his study of the painting as a framed image, Stoichita writes: "The frame separates the image from anything that is nonimage. It defines what is framed as a meaningful world as opposed to the outside—the frame, which is simply the world experienced. We should, however, ask ourselves: To which of the two worlds does the frame belong?"[31]

In Jansson's picture book, metapictorial effects as well as visual splitting strategies are used to investigate the ontological status of the work. Allusions

---

[29] Lawrence Sterne, *The Life and Opinions of Tristram Shandy, Gentleman* (1759-1767), 6th book.
[30] See Patricia Waugh, *Metafiction: The Theory and Practice of self-Conscious Fiction* (London: Routledge, 1984). For metafiction more specifically in children's literature see David Lewis, "The Constructedness of Texts: Picture Books and the Metafictive," in *Only Connect: Readings on Children's Literature* ed. Sheila Egoff (Toronto: Oxford U.P., 1996), 131-146; and Maria Nikolajeva and Carole Scott, *How Picturebooks Work*, (New York: Garland, 2001), 211-241.
[31] Stoichita, 30.

and intertextual references to literature and art are used in an ironic and humorous manner. As in Dante's *Inferno*, the main character finds himself in a dark forest in the beginning of the poem, enters a gate to the underworld, meets frightening beasts of impressive scale and quality, and almost drowns—not unlike *Alice in Wonderland*—in a sea of tears.

However, the terrifying monsters are ambivalent in Jansson's story. The cleaning Hemulen (a male figure dressed in an apron), draws Moomin accidentally into the mouth of the vacuum cleaner. He is merely cleaning and seems totally unaware of the distress he causes. And yet, the strange creatures they meet are imposing in their size. In fact, Hemulen seems gigantic in this scene, large enough to swallow Moomin and his friends in his vacuum cleaner. The scene is amusing but also claustrophobic. We see Moomin spiralling forward inside the narrow hose of the vacuum cleaner, visualised as a cross-section image. Even the text becomes more uncontrolled and unstable. The bumpy ride is described with increasing intensity and anxiety: The text lines describing their movement are bent and whirling uncontrollably, corresponding to Moomin's helpless situation.

The transitions between reality and imagination—the metafictitional aspects—parody, and the hyperbolic features as well as elements of horror suggest a connection to romanticism. If one reads the story as a performance, as a theatre act, the structure of repeated frightful and terrifying scenes that are abruptly interrupted and cut off becomes visible. The dramatically illuminated settings—the shallow perspective and flat, geometrical forms that partly cover each other—create strangely scenic scenery. The spatial organization and structure of the landscape resembles a theatre stage where the stage set is changed in every scene without actual pictorial depth, yet creating an illusion of three-dimensionality as we observe layers of pictures overlapping.[32] Theatre as a location for magic and carnival escapades is frequently used by Jansson. In *Moominsummer Madness* (1954), the family is stranded on an abandoned theatre house during a flood. Here one of the characters tries to explain the concept of theatre to the unenlightened Moomin family who has never heard of such a thing: "'A theatre is the most important sort of house in the world, because that's where people are shown what they could be if they wanted, and what they'd like to be if they dared to and what they really are.' 'A reformatory,' said Moominmamma, astonished."[33]

Theatre plays and fantastic adventures through acting is a common stylistic

---

[32]Compare with Drucker's discussion of artist's books that use the book conceptually to duplicate the spatial quality of performance or using the page as a theatrical space, chapter twelve.

[33] Tove Jansson, *Farlig midsommar* (1954), trans. Thomas Warburton, *Moominsummer Madness* (London: Ernest Benn, 1955).

device in children's literature.[34] This is expressed in Jansson's story through actions that have performative qualities, but also through a somewhat sporadic narrative structure. In the final scene in *The Book about Moomin, Mymble and Little My,* all the small creatures from previous scenes in the book are drawn together. Like an ensemble of actors, they witness the concluding scene of homecoming. Peculiar looking creatures from the earlier nightmarish scenes are now gathered peacefully in Moominmamma's garden, witnessing Moomitroll's return home. Even the transformation of the environment is noteworthy. We have moved from the uncontrolled and undomesticated dreamlike landscape towards a controlled, stabile, and cultivated setting—the garden. The next step from the scene in the garden is that we are transported indoors, inside the Moomin house. The book is provided with a happy end, as always in Tove Jansson's books, as Moomintroll finally concludes his task, brings home the milk bucket (although the milk has gone sour), and is reunited with his mother.

As the story comes to its end, the implied, literary flow of time stops. The graphic illusion of proposed three-dimensional space is suddenly gone. The flat surface of the paper now lacks volume, depth, and perspective. The endpaper shows the characters turned towards us, pointing out the fact that the final hole is too small to get through. The story is concluded:

> This hole–the very last, you see–they can't get through–it's much too wee.
> We'll stay here in this book, and why? Cause we are too big!!! said Little My.

Until now, panoramic sceneries are used to show landscapes reaching toward the back of the pictorial space. The indoor setting portrays, however, an enclosed space. By separating the inside from the outside, the fictive is separated from reality. Little My is once again the one that signals the fictionality of the fiction. As I have discussed earlier, some illustrations emphasise the different levels of image and play with the concept of page. Towards the end of the story, the boundary between the fictional world of the book and the real world of the reader is called attention to. As we close the covers, we see a closed back door with the sign "will be back soon." We are suddenly outside the Moomin house and on our way out of the fictional sphere. The story has reached its end and we have now stepped outside its territory. In a similar manner to the gaps, the covers are used to call attention to the boarders of fiction and reality. The transparency of the picture surface is accentuated.

---

[34]Perry Nodelman uses the term "stage pictures" to describe the scenic, stage-like character of the spatial construction in some illustrations, *Words about Pictures* (Athens: Univ. of Georgia Press, 1988), 155. See also, Amy E Spaulding's *The Page as a Stage Set: Storyboard Picture Books*, (London: Scarecrow, 1995).

Similar to the frames of a painting, the book covers define and separate fiction from reality. Emphasising the inside, as well as the empty parts of the image field, is to distinguish the unified field of the closed composition of the fictional world. The gaps functions not only as doorways or as a linked spatial entity related to the work in a metapictorial and self reflecting manner; it also points out the connection to the world outside the work. Similar to the round window on the front cover, the last gap opens up the interior of the work to the outside. We close the book and are presented with the image of the closed front door. The key is hanging on the wall, suggesting that although we are now left outside the covers of the picture book, excluded from the fictional sphere, the reader is always welcome to enter the story anew.

To emphasize the inside to the extent that it is regarded in tension with its framing, the book covers, is to embed the inside as an image within an image. By pointing at the conventions of reading, on the concept of the book and the page, one is pointing out the book as a whole and focusing on its materiality. This kind of focus on the material qualities of the medium draws attention to the physical form of the picture book: to the relationship between text and illustration, book covers, the specific focus on turning of the pages, as well as other paratextual features. Even the materiality of the verbal text is focused on through the use of layout in an experimental manner.

In my analysis of Jansson's experimental picture book, I have discussed how the book's tactile and material qualities are used to transform the spatial structure. The material qualities of the medium are used to give the spatial construction of the picture book a scenic, stage-like quality. Manipulation of the book's material qualities, in the form of perforated pages or through metafictional play with different levels of pictorial representation, furthermore interrogates the concept of the image and the page. The intertextual and metafictional methods used by Jansson through her entire production involve humorous philosophical examination of literature and art, of fiction and reality. Playing with the fictional boarders in this manner can take place outside normal structures of space and time, but it may also transform its appearance and organize space and time in unexpected ways.

CHAPTER THREE

JERRY SPINELLI'S *STARGIRL* AS CONTEMPORARY GOSPEL: GOOD NEWS FOR A WORLD OF ADOLESCENT CONFORMITY

BETH COOLEY

[*Editor's note*: The material in this article was originally presented at a panel for the 59th annual conference of the Rocky Mountain Modern Language Association at Coeur d'Alene, Idaho, in 2005.]

Stargirl, Jerry Spinelli's novel of heroic nonconformity, is a slim and simple volume even by Young Adult standards. Recognized by *Publishers Weekly, The New York Times,* ALA, and others as a "best" novel of the year in 2000, this graceful narrative follows the rise and fall of Stargirl Caraway, a seventeen year old non-conformist. While this novel deals with none of the so-called "topical relevancies" of adolescent life—substance abuse, parental neglect, sexuality, disability, in short, standard fare of the "problem novel"—it clearly has relevance for the contemporary adolescent reader. If, as Richard Peck notes, "the drug of choice in adolescence is conformity,"[35] we might see *Stargirl* as detoxifying, a novel of nonconformity that speaks to "the conventional children of privilege and permissiveness,"[36] and which "questions provincial pieties without belittling the problems or telling [conventional middle class readers] they don't have any."[37] And yet, even as it explores the "provincial pieties" of "normal" high school society, the novel reaches beyond the realm of adolescent realism. When examined through the lens of biblical typology, *Stargirl* reveals deeper layers. The immediate story of Stargirl Caraway and the locale of Mica, Arizona (a name which ironically evokes Old Testament prophesy as it

---

[35]Richard Peck, *Love and Death at the Mall: Teaching and Writing for the Literate Young* (New York: Delacorte Press, 1994), 84.
[36]Richard Peck, "Problem Novels for Readers Without Any," in *Reading Their World,* ed. V. Monseau and G. Salvner (Portsmouth, NH: Boynton/Cook; Heinemann, 1992), 76.
[37]Ibid., 76.

simultaneously suggests glitter and flakiness), are invested with allegorical, even mythical significance. When encoded with biblical allusion *Stargirl* becomes a contemporary gospel, good news about the possibility of living an authentic, creative life, even in high school.

Reviewers of Spinelli's novel have disparagingly described the protagonist as "too good to be true," a "contemporary Pollyanna" who has "no shadows to contour her character."[38] In their apparent search for a female counterpart to Maniac Magee, these reviewers fail to recognize that Stargirl, "larger-than-life" and "hard to pin down,"[39] might best be understood as the protagonist of a millennial gospel narrated by her most devoted, and sometimes most mystified, disciple, Leo Borlock. Students of literature are, of course, familiar with the myriad Christ figures found in the western canon. From Ahab to Benjy Compson to Bilbo Baggins, they abound. Sacvan Bercovitch and others have explored the "imitation of Christ" theme in American literature from its Colonial beginnings in the seventeenth century to the present. My own undergraduate literary training seemed, at times, to rest primarily on the ability to find Jesus in every text, and *Stargirl* provides another opportunity. Simultaneously, however, the novel begs us to recognize and then modify, if not deconstruct, Stargirl as traditional Christ figure. If, as Michael Cart suggests, we view the history of the Young Adult novel as "a series of inspired exercises in iconoclasm, of taboo busting, of shibboleth shattering,"[40] *Stargirl* presents a historical moment. While Stargirl is herself a messianic iconoclast, the novel is equally iconoclastic. Both character and novel advocate kindness, honesty, empathy, truth, certainly timeless values that adolescents need to learn, and yet *Stargirl* never becomes didactic. Stargirl moves beyond the often worn-out cliché of the suffering messiah and teaches a new lesson in how to actively survive in a hypocritical and conformist world. By looking first at the parallels between Stargirl and the literary Christ figure and then locating points of departure between the two, we both recognize the traditional values afforded by biblical reference and discern the novel's break with biblical convention in an attempt to replace the passivity often attributed to the self-denying Christ figure with creative self-definition.

Many of Stargirl's parallels to Jesus of Nazareth are perhaps obvious. To begin with, Stargirl's most recent name suggests the famous star of Bethlehem, harbinger of the prophesied Christ. Furthermore, the fact that she has taken so many monikers parallels Jesus' own list of names, from Messiah, to King of the

---

[38]R. S., review of *Stargirl* by Jerry Spinelli, *Horn Book* 76, no. 4: 456.
[39]Jerry Spinelli, qtd. in Jennifer Brown, "Jerry Spinelli, Homer on George Street," *Publisher's Weekly* 247, no. 29: 68.
[40]Michael Cart, *From Romance to Realism: Fifty Years of Growth and Change in Young Adult Literature* (New York: Harper Collins, 1995), 184.

Jews, to Son of God, to Christ. Similarly, although Stargirl has no John the Baptist, her fame precedes her, and Leo Borlock, the narrator of Spinelli's gospel, experiences her presence in the form of a gift before she makes her first appearance at Mica High School. On his fourteenth birthday, Leo receives from an unidentified giver a necktie illustrated with porcupines; the number of porcupines on the tie is, perhaps significantly, three. Only after watching Stargirl perform anonymous and random acts of kindness among the common people in the Arizona Desert does Leo figure out where the gift came from. Stargirl's mercurial rise to popularity also parallels Jesus' growing influence in Palestine and surrounding areas. She first catches the town of Mica's attention with her unconventional and uninhibited behavior, and before long has a large band of followers. "We honored her by imitation," Leo remembers and notes the town's run on ukuleles and pet rats, Stargirl's signature attributes.[41] Among other things, Stargirl is honored and admired for her stunning gift of oratory. Like Jesus's preaching, Stargirl's impromptu speeches hold audiences captive. "Such was the acclamation we gave her," Leo says recalling their rapt attention; he adds, "But we also gave something to ourselves."[42]

In losing themselves in Stargirl, the teens of Mica High School find themselves. Leo compares his classmates to desert mud frogs who hibernate in dried mud until the rains come: "It was wonderful to see, wonderful to be in the middle of: we mud frogs awakening all around. We were awash in tiny attentions. Small gestures, words, empathies thought to be extinct came to life."[43] Unable to account for Stargirl's influence, Leo describes the phenomenon as "a rebellion *for* rather than against. For ourselves. For the dormant mud frogs we had been for so long." Like Jesus, Stargirl is mobbed with popularity and emulation, and her disciple is ecstatic. He exclaims to his friend and mentor, Archie, "It's a miracle." "Best hope it's not," Archie says bringing both Leo and the novel back to reality. "The trouble with miracles is, they don't last long."[44] As Archie predicts, Stargirl's influence doesn't last—it can't. Like Jesus, she breaks too many rules, inevitably infuriating not only Hillari Kimball, a sort of high school Pharisee and Stargirl's arch-nemesis, but also her most devoted followers who suddenly find her brand of kindness invasive and even improper. Just as quickly as she rose to popularity, Stargirl falls.

Stargirl's Christlike rise and fall from almost universal celebrity and popularity are matched with other messianic qualities. One of these qualities is her elusiveness. Leo describes her as "hard to pin down," and wonders more

---

[41]Jerry Spinelli, *Stargirl* (New York: Knopf, 2000), 38.
[42]Ibid., 39.
[43]Ibid., 40.
[44]Ibid., 41-42.

than once, "Is she real?" With characteristic cynicism, his best friend, Kevin, says "she better be fake."[45] What would Mica do if she were, in fact, genuine? By novel's end Leo asks the question again. "It seems like a dream," he tells Archie, then asks, "Was she really here? Who was she? Was she real?" echoing questions that have surrounded the historic as well as the mythic Jesus for centuries.[46] Ultimately both Leo and the reader see that Stargirl is real, human, one of us, and yet she is a miracle, a mystery, "the rabbit in the hat."[47] Failing to comprehend her actions, Leo at one point accuses her of running for saint and consequently misses the essence of Stargirl: her humanity. As Archie tries to explain, "every once in a while someone comes along who is a little more primitive than the rest of us, a little closer to our beginnings, a little more in touch with the stuff we're made of." She seems to be in touch "with something that the rest of us are missing."[48] Paradoxically, her quintessential humanity seems to border on the divine. As if to reinforce this mystical quality, Jerry Spinelli himself has described Stargirl as a kind of alpha and omega. In a 2000 interview he says, "I think she perhaps resides in more than just this moment. I see her as having come from the past and anticipating the future, at the same time participating fully in the present."[49] She was, will be and is: the word became flesh for those, like Leo Borlock, who have ears to hear.

Leo, who follows her into the desert and then falls in love with her testifies, "She taught me to revel. She taught me to wonder. She taught me to laugh. . . . She saw things. I had not known there was so much to see."[50] In one of the longest scenes in the book, she leads Leo to a special place, a place she recognizes as sacred. She instructs Leo to take off his shoes; then she sits in the lotus position and waits for enchantment. "So what do we do," Leo asks. "That's the secret," she replies. "We do nothing." In a Socratic dialog between teacher and disciple, she echoes several of Christianity's most paradoxical teachings. We have eyes and ears but don't see or hear; in order to find ourselves we must lose ourselves. Leo, like most disciples, has trouble attaining enlightenment, but Stargirl, "her lips faintly smiling," her skin golden in the desert light, is "serenity" itself.[51] Here she is perhaps more traditional Buddha than Christ; even so, she has attained spiritual peace. Ironically, Leo feels a "pang of jealousy that she could be sitting next to [him] and not know it. That

---

[45]Ibid., 9.
[46]Ibid., 176.
[47]Ibid., 181.
[48]Ibid., 102.
[49]Spinelli, qtd. in Jennifer Brown, "Jerry Spinelli," 69.
[50]Spinelli, *Stargirl*, 107.
[51]Ibid., 93.

she could be somewhere most wonderful and [he] could not be there."[52] Yet by simply being in Stargirl's presence, he is able to find a modicum of peace in the desert.

Despite her wisdom and charisma, Stargirl, like Christ, becomes the archetypal scapegoat. She is sacrificed to conventionality, crucified on the cross of mediocrity. The catalyst for this scapegoating is Stargirl's completely unconventional and radically Christian act of "giving comfort to the enemy," an injured Sun Valley basketball player during a game.[53] As a cheerleader for the Mica High School Electrons, Stargirl commits heresy, blasphemy, and her act of kindness is enough to provoke public shunning. However, the change in people's reactions toward her has been a long time coming: "They said she thought she was some kind of saint. . . and that she was better than the rest of us. They said she wanted everyone else to feel guilty for not being as nice and wonderful as she was." Echoing Kevin's prediction that she's "fake," they label Stargirl "a phoney." Stargirl, of course, escapes any physical harm; she is not literally crucified, but she is shunned. Leo is at a loss to explain the power of conformists to his surprisingly naive messiah: "This group thing. . . it's very strong. It's probably an instinct," he says. When Stargirl fails to understand, he states simply, "We live in a world of them."[54] Two days later Stargirl vanishes. Typologically, she has been crucified dead and is buried. When she re-enters the doors of Mica High School, however, she is not resurrected but still confined within the tomb of popular culture. Her standard becomes the fictitious "Evelyn Everyone," and her slogan, "What would Evelyn Do?" ironically echoes, "What would Jesus do?" She forsakes her rat, her ukulele, and her cosmic name for designer clothes and nail polish and, Leo tells us, looks "magnificently, wonderfully, gloriously ordinary."[55]

Our reading of Stargirl's interment within the tomb of mediocrity and descent into the hell of conformity might also be informed by John Stephens's essay "Construction of Female Selves in Adolescent Fiction: Makeovers as Metonym." Adapting Judith Butler's distinction between *expression* and *performativeness* in the creation of gendered selves, Stephens sees the first as connected to "identity as stable or a locus of agency," and the second as "identity as the performance of attributes" which are "generated within time and place" and imitate a superficial social ideal.[56] Ironically, Stargirl's makeover is of the second kind. Frequently the "makeover in teen fiction" is "a central

---

[52]Ibid., 94.
[53]Ibid., 127.
[54]Ibid., 137-38.
[55]Ibid., 140.
[56]John Stephens, "Constructions of Female Selves in Adolescent Fiction: Makeovers as Metonym," *Papers* 9, no.1 (1999), 5.

metonym for growth."[57]   It can signify positive transformation and self actualization, or it can "constitute a wrong movement which comes to be identified as such." Readers are quick to see Stargirl's makeover into Evelyn Everyone as "cautionary." They recognize this as a "Cinderella" makeover "whereby the character involved does the job herself. . . and slips further and further into narcissism as she produces an inauthentic self."[58] We see that, as is so often the case with conformity-addicted teens, "performance has occluded expression." Having "shaped herself as a performance of a particular social image in discord with her interior stage of being,"[59] Stargirl remains entombed in fashionable conformity for much longer than three days. Ironically reinforced by her disciple, who not only fails to recognize her entombment for what it is but finds her performativeness "wonderful," Stargirl's story diverges from Christ's who is mourned by his followers. As the plot again converges with biblical typology, however, Stargirl is finally resurrected. She realizes that transforming herself into an Evelyn Everyone named Susan (the name she was christened with) does not fulfill her. Nor does it allow her to fulfill her destiny as rebel with a very good cause.

Another point of divergence between Stargirl and Christ involves the ultimate act of sacrifice. If Christ died for the salvation of unworthy sinners, Stargirl is sacrificed, or sacrifices herself, on the cross of conformity for a much smaller, more conventional and more realistic population, Leo Borlock, her boyfriend. After she has disappeared from Mica for good at the end of the novel, Archie points out to Leo, "She did it for you, you know. . . . Gave up her self for a while there. She loved you that much."[60] When Leo admits that he knows this, Archie replies, "No you don't. You can't know yet." Was Leo worthy of Stargirl's ultimate self sacrifice? Is anyone worthy of that kind of love? This question is left unanswered, but another question, perhaps more relevant to the purpose of the novel, is answered when the stone of conformity is rolled away. That question, should anyone sacrifice herself for the approval of her peers, even the most elect peer, is answered with a resounding "no." For those who insist upon recognizing indiscriminate sacrifice as the primary attribute of the literary Christ figure, Stargirl refuses to fit the mold. Iconoclastic to the end, she refuses to be categorized, even by literary scholars.

Susan Caraway (aka Evelyn Everyone) emerges as Stargirl again but in a rarified state. She has moved beyond any performative desire to conform. She has even moved beyond pleasing Leo at the risk of self-erasure. In fact, she is more herself, more expressive, than ever. Her final appearance at the Ocotillo

---

[57]Ibid., 6.
[58]Ibid., 7.
[59]Ibid., 9.
[60]Spinelli, *Stargirl*, 178.

ball cements her place in Mica mythology. She arrives in a bicycle side car driven by Dori Dilson, who is cross-dressed in a white tuxedo. Dori is not her date, however, but only the chauffeur who presents "this three-wheeled bouquet" to Mica's teens.[61] Details about Stargirl's dress, her jewelry, and her hair blur in the many accounts of her splendor. She is alone, an outsider still, yet she is "complete" and looks into the eyes of her classmates, "smiling as if she knows them, as if they have shared grand and special things."[62] More elusive, more miraculous than ever, she mesmerizes the ball-goers and leads them bunny hopping through the desert, a place often signifying spiritual transformation in biblical typology. Returning her followers safe but forever changed to the dance floor she is confronted by Hillari Kimball, arch Pharisee of high school conformity. "You ruin everything," Hillari says and slaps her face. Rather than simply turn the other cheek, Stargirl kisses Hillari, ironically suggesting Judas rather than Christ. With this kiss she rejects Hillari and all she stands for while at the same time forgiving her. Then she disappears forever, leaving Leo to tell her story.

Like Christ's disciples, Leo is an ordinary person whose life has been transformed by an inspiring individual. As with traditional gospel narrators, his tone is sometimes one of looking back on amazing events in awed near-comprehension. What has been interpreted as "an unnecessary adult perspective"[63] actually provides the distance necessary for contemplating and relating Stargirl's significance. Leo's reverence and devotion are tempered by his willingness to at least try to portray all aspects of Stargirl's character objectively, even the parts he can't understand or admire. Again, this connects him to the gospel writers who (although they were not eye-witnesses as Leo is) seem to be recording what remains in many ways a mystery, but a mystery they are willing to accept. By the end of the novel, Stargirl has inexplicably vanished, leaving Leo to spread the good news of her coming and evidence of her continued presence in the world. "Was she real?" Leo asks, and Archie answers, "Yes." That is the "good news" (Archie's words), the gospel. Mica High School will be forever changed. Archie calls her "the universal solvent," "the recycler of our garbage," washing away the sins of conformity and leaving generations of followers who do much in remembrance of her.[64] A ukulele player accompanies the Mica Electrons marching band, a small group of Electron fans cheers for the opposing team, and Mica is a kinder place. At the end of the novel Leo is clearly waiting for Stargirl's second coming. Although,

---

[61]Ibid., 168.
[62]Ibid., 169.
[63]Sharon Grover, review of *Stargirl* by Jerry Spinelli, *School Library Journal* 46, no. 8: 190.
[64]Spinelli, *Stargirl*, 185.

fifteen years later, he has no family of his own, he does not feel alone. "I know that I am being watched," he says. Furthermore, only a month before, he received a gift-wrapped birthday package in the mail. "It was a porcupine necktie."[65]

Like Leo, young readers, too, can experience the good news of Stargirl whom Spinelli himself describes as "emulatable and not beyond the reach of today's kid."[66] Of course many writers and critics of YA novels focus on their potential to provide what William Dean Myers has called "strategies for living."[67] Richard Peck has eloquently described successful YA literature as "a celebration of the individual sharpened at a time in life and history when the young individual is under particular fire and needs encouragement well beyond the needs of most adult readers."[68] Similarly, Sandy Asher sees YA novels as potentially giving readers "words to explain yourself, words you can use to create your own life, to recognize your options and to make your choices. To separate as an individual and to reconnect as a member of the human race."[69] However, she also warns against "bibliotherapy," a system which "doses young readers with medicine and therapy and requires the breaking down of novels into utilitarian parts."[70] A typological reading of *Stargirl* should not get in the way of the readers' personal response to the text. Nor should it reduce the novel to fundamentalist didacticism and set the teacher up as "Sole Living Authorit[y] expected to dish out the One True Vision of a book."

In *Exploding the Myths: The Truth about Teens and Reading*, Marc Aronson critiques what he calls "the moral instruction gang" of recent YA writers, and makes a distinction between two kinds of current YA novels.[71] The first he describes as "a kind of mini-Bible that serves as babysitter for older children"[72] and offers "predigested morals and fake realities that readers will soon see through."[73] The second kind of novels are "books that take readers to discover new realities in themselves and derive their moral quality from their

---

[65]Ibid., 186.
[66]Spinelli, qtd. in Jennifer Brown, "Jerry Spinelli," 69.
[67]William Dean Meyers, qtd. in Jean Brown and Elaine Stephens, *Teaching Young Adult Literature: Sharing the Connection* (New York: Wadsworth, 1995), 6.
[68]Peck, *Love and Death at the Mall,* 158.
[69]Sandy Asher, "What About Now? What About Here? What About Me?" in *Reading Their World,* ed. V. Monseau and G. Salvner (Portsmouth, NH: Boynton/Cook; Heinemann, 1992), 82.
[70]Sandy Asher, "Ride the Horse in the Direction It's Going," in *Authors' Insights,* ed. Donald Gallo (Portsmouth, NH: Boynton/Cook; Heinemann, 1991), 14.
[71]Aronson, Marc, *Exploding the Myths: The Truth About Teens and Reading* (Lanham, MD: Scarecrow, 2001), 115.
[72]Ibid., 70.
[73]Ibid., 83.

unpredictable depths." *Stargirl* is clearly a novel of the second category and should be read and taught as such. Rather than the didactic "mini-bible" that Aronson condemns, it is a gospel with all the paradoxes and mysteries of the road to enlightenment. This road eventually leads to good news about the best adolescents can be—creative nonconformists, outsiders, and rebels, not rebels *against*, but rebels *for*: for joy, for empathy, for kindness in a desert of stasis and convention. Star people.

CHAPTER FOUR

REHABILITATING THE WOLF: INTERTEXTUALITY AND VISUAL ALLUSION IN GEOFFROY DE PENNART'S PICTURE BOOKS

DEBORAH MITTS-SMITH

[*Editor's note*: The material in this article was originally presented at a panel for the 59th annual conference of the Rocky Mountain Modern Language Association at Coeur d'Alene, Idaho, in 2005.]

In recent years the rehabilitation of the Big Bad Wolf of folk and fairy tales has become a common and popular motif in children's books. Typically it has been accomplished either through role reversal, as in Eugene Trivizas and Helen Oxenbury's *The Three Little Wolves and the Big Bad Pig*, or through a change in perspective, as in Jon Scieszka and Lane Smith's *The True Story of the Three Little Pigs*, which relates the tale from the point of view of the wolf. Geoffroy de Pennart's series of French picture books featuring a bevy of wolves uses the old tales to redefine the wolf in new ways. Through a web of humor, intertextuality, and hypertextuality, Pennart conjures up, disrupts, and undoes the tales. Mirroring the relatively recent rehabilitation of the wolf in ecology and society, Pennart transforms the wolf from a metaphor of human predation and gluttony to one of benign and even admirable qualities. A close examination of *Le loup est revenu!* *[The Wolf Has Returned!]*, *Je suis revenu* [I Have Returned], *Le loup sentimental* *[The Sentimental Wolf]*, *Le loup, la chèvre et les 7 chevreaux*, *[The Wolf, the Goat and the 7 Kids]*, and *Chapeau rond rouge* *[Little Red Hat]* reveals the ways in which Pennart's reworking of traditional stories, characters, and settings reflect contemporary attitudes towards wolves.

Pennart's wolf stories, while drawing inspiration from traditional wolf tales and fables, exist in a narrative space outside that of the traditional stories. Two of his works, *Le loup, la chèvre, et les 7 chevreaux* and *Chapeau rond rouge* parody their more traditional counterparts, while three others, *Le loup est revenu!*, *Je suis revenu*, and *Le loup sentimental*, are populated with characters and settings from several Western European wolf fables and tales. Each of these familiar characters or settings recalls and evokes the stories that they represent. In this way the characters and settings act as intertextual elements, giving voice to multiple texts within a story. By bringing together characters from several fables and tales, Pennart adds another layer of intertextuality to his stories. As Gianni Rodari, who described such jumbles of fairy tale characters as a "Fairy Tale Salad Mix," suggested, subjecting stories and characters "to this treatment, even the images that are most constantly used[,] appear to take on a new life, to blossom again, and to bear fruit and flowers in unexpected ways."[74] The mixed cast of characters in Pennart's wolf series not only evokes the traditional narratives that they represent, but also the identity of the wolf. At the same time, their new encounters with the wolf outside the context of the fables and tales result not only in re-writing their exchanges with the wolf, but also in transforming the wolf himself. The wolf's identity is evoked and almost in the same instance dismantled by these hypertextual and intertextual allusions.

In *Le loup est revenu!*, news that the Wolf has returned puts his usual victims into a panic. On the cover of the book, a rabbit, aptly named Rabbit, is depicted reading the newspaper announcing the Wolf's return. The story begins with a knock on the door that sends Rabbit into a state of alarm. It is not only Rabbit's terror, but the reader's prior knowledge that renders the knock ominous. In a pattern that is repeated almost to end, Rabbit opens the door to find not the Wolf, but the Three Pigs, the Mother Goat and her seven kids, the Little Lamb, Peter and the duck, and Little Red Riding Hood. As more and more characters gather at Rabbit's house, each knock raises the level of suspense. In between knocks, Rabbit and his guests relax. True to the characterization of the traditional stories and fables, most of the characters come to Rabbit's house in a fearful state. Only Peter and Little Red Riding Hood arrive unafraid. Peter, reprising his role from *Peter and the Wolf*, is hunting the Wolf. Little Red Riding Hood, on the other hand, arrives in complete ignorance. Not only has she *not* heard the news about the Wolf's return, but she is also unaware that her grandmother has moved and so knocks on Rabbit's door by mistake. As Sandra L. Beckett suggests, "the innocence and naivety of the classic heroine is parodied in this comical scene that suggests that the little girl is illiterate and rather stupid, as she stands smiling blankly and holding out her basket of cakes and butter, thinking she's at her grandmother's door."[75]

When they all are there, Rabbit decides that they should take advantage of the situation and have dinner together. As they prepare the food and the table,

---

[74]Gianni Rodari, *The Grammar of Fantasy* trans. Jack Zipes (New York: Teachers & Writers Collaborative, 1996), 38.
[75]Sanrda L. Beckett, *Recycling Red Riding Hood*, Children's Literature and Culture, vol. 23, ser. ed. Jack Zipes (New York: Routledge, 2002), 286.

there is one last knock on the door. The powerful knock, "BOUM! BOUM! BOUM!," immediately distinguishes the new arrival from the earlier ones. Rabbit's response is also different. As if having forgotten the reason why these visitors are there, Rabbit responds to the knock with « 'Tiens,' dit monsieur Lapin, l'air étonné. Nous n'attendons plus personne !' » ("Hold on!" says Mr. Rabbit in an astonished air. "We aren't expecting anyone else.").[76] It is of course, the Wolf.

Up until this moment, our knowledge of the Wolf comes from two sources: the newspapers stories of the Wolf's return, and the tales and fables featuring wolves. With the arrival of each new character, save Little Red Riding Hood, comes another newspaper bearing yet more information about the Wolf and his intentions. As such, each new knock on the door not only increases the tension, but also the presence of the Wolf. Rabbit's paper features not only a story reporting the Wolf has returned, but also that he is in good physical condition [« Je suis en plein forme! »] and has a recipe for rabbit in plum sauce [« lapin au pruneaux. »].[77] The Three Pigs' paper, *Le Tire-Bouchon* [The Cork Screw] also features an article on the Wolf return, while in the Goats' paper, *LE CROTTIN DE CHAVIGNOL* [Goat's Milk Cheese], the Wolf promises to pay a visit to his friend the Goat and her charming family. Photographs accompanying the articles render the Wolf present while depicting him in poses (smiling with a napkin around his neck, showing off his muscles, and licking his lips) that parody his dangerous tendencies.

The fear of the Wolf's return takes on greater significance in light of the texts surrounding the Wolf's role in traditional tales and fables. In other words, our reading of the newspaper blurbs is also influenced by the reader's knowledge of the wolf tales. The presence of such characters as the Three Pigs, the Little Lamb, the Mother Goat and her 7 kids, Peter and Little Red Riding Hood—and the texts they carry with them—identify and define the threat posed by the Wolf's wicked nature. The Wolf that has returned is the one who blows down houses, dons disguises, and deceives lambs, goats, and little girls in order to satisfy his gluttonous urges. What is often overlooked, however, is that even though the Wolf sometimes wins as in Charles Perrault's *Le petit chaperon rouge*, he often ends up being captured or dying at the end of the tales.

When at last the knock on the door announces the Wolf's arrival, Rabbit and his guests, instead of fleeing, throw themselves on him.[78] United, these characters are able to do what none is able to do in his or her own story: physically overcome the Wolf. Known mainly for his strength, the overpowering of the Wolf by his usual victims diminishes his power over them

---

[76]Geoffroy de Pennart, *Le loup est revenu!* (Paris: L'Ecole des loisirs, 1994), 27.
[77]Ibid., 5-7.
[78]Ibid., 29-30.

and changes our view of him as a threat. Appropriately enough, Pennart depicts the Wolf in a submissive position on his back with his belly exposed. After the Rabbit declares that they, the Wolf's prey, are no longer afraid of him, Rabbit proposes a truce: they will share their meal with the Wolf, if he promises to be nice and "tell them scary wolf stories" [« raconter des histoires de loup qui font peur »].[79] This last request alludes directly to popular European wolf tales from which this story gains its meaning as well as to Pennart's story itself: Pennart's story is a scary, if humorous, wolf tale that derives its energy and tensions from the traditional characters of scary wolf tales.

In *Je suis revenu*, Pennart revisits *Le loup est revenu!*, rewriting it from the point of view of the Wolf. By focusing directly on the Wolf and his actions prior to arriving at Rabbit's house, Pennart adds yet another layer of intertextuality to his story. Copies of the Wolf's letters to the newspapers litter the endpapers: "It is with great pleasure that I announce my return to the area!!!! I am in great shape!!! Do you know that I greatly love rabbits !!!! Besides which, I also know an excellent recipe for rabbit in plum sauce.!!!!" [« J'ai le grand plaisir de vous annoncer mon retour dans la région !!! Je suis en très grande pleine forme !!! Savez-vous que j'aime énormément les lapins !!! Je connais d'ailleurs une excellente recette de lapin aux pruneaux. »].[80] These letters are the source of the headlines, photographs, and captions that fueled the panic in *Le loup est revenu!*.

The Wolf's story begins with the Wolf asking us if we recognize him; and as if to assuage any doubts we may have, he tells us: "I am the wolf!"[« Je suis le loup! »]. As he exercises, the Wolf declares: "I am back in the area, even stronger, even more intelligent. A truly bad wolf!" [« Me voici de retour dans la région, encore plus costaud, encore plus intelligent. Un vrai méchant loup, quoi ! »]. On the wall behind him is his source of inspiration: a portrait gallery of his *vieux amis* [old friends] Rabbit, Little Red Riding Hood, Peter, the Three Pigs, the Goat family and the Lamb.[81]

The plot follows Wolf as he returns to his old haunts in search of his *vieux amis*. As the Wolf in *Le loup est revenu!* was at first only present through textual and visual allusions, so the Pigs, Goats, Lamb, Little Red Riding Hood and Peter in *Je suis revenu* are at first only present through textual and visual allusions. Pennart's use of allusions adds to the excitement of the stories. The combination of the Wolf, his banter, and settings strewn with visual reminders of these characters and their stories seemingly confirms the Wolf's gluttonous intentions. Arriving at the brick home of the Three Pigs, there is a heap of straw and a pile of sticks. The Wolf comments: "Ha, I recognize this place. Puff, the

---

[79]Ibid., 32.
[80]Pennart, *Je suis revenue* (Paris: L'Ecole des loisirs, 1999), 4-5.
[81]Ibid., 9; 10; 11.

house of straw, puff, the house of sticks." [« Ha, ha je reconnais cet endroit. Pfff, la maison de paille, pfff, la maison de bois. »]. "Do you know what I call the house of bricks? I call it the butcher's shop and it is here where I will do my grocery shopping". [« Vous savez comment j'appelle la maison de brique ? Je l'appelle la charcuterie et c'est la que je vais faire mes courses, ha, ha, ha ! »]. [82] But this time the Wolf has come prepared to deal with the house of bricks. No more huffing and puffing. Instead, using a set of master keys and a crowbar to tackle the lock, the Wolf brags that he is a professional. When the Wolf enters the home, there are three chairs for the three porcine brothers, a copy of the song *Qui a peur du grand mechant loup?* [*Who's Afraid of the Big Bad Wolf?*], and an image of Wolf super-imposed on the dart board, but no pigs.

As he moves from house to house in search of his old friends, the Wolf finds each place deserted. It is only when he overhears the worried conversation of Little Red Riding Hood's parents that he is led to the Grandmother's house. When he arrives, he, like the little girl in red, discovers that the Grandmother has moved. His disappointment, however, is short-lived when he realizes that the new resident is a Mr. Rabbit: "Nothing better than a saddle of rabbit for a wolf who is very, very hungry..." [(« Rien de quel bon râble de lapin pour un loup qui a vraiment très très faim... »].[83]

The ending of *Le loup est revenu!* is now repeated from the wolf's perspective. As the Wolf says, he had barely made a move when they jumped him. Accepting their invitation to dine with them, the Wolf is last seen sitting at the table, eating cake with his *vieux amis.*

Pennart's titles indicate that the wolf has come back. But from where? As their titles and plots suggest, these stories take place after the traditional tales and fables end. But how can the Wolf, who dies or is captured in these tales, come back? Given that the first of these stories, *Le loup est revenu!*, was published in the early 1990s, around the time when real wolves, which had been extinct in France since the 1920s, returned to France, it is a headline that could have easily reflected French reality. Like the Wolf in Pennart's stories, the wolf in France has come back from extinction. Read against this background, the request for scary wolf tales and the Wolf's declarations that he is not so bad take on yet another level of meaning. Within the current context of favorable public attitudes towards wolves, the traditional tales have lost some of their edge. Pennart's light-hearted picture books help to complete the transformation of the Big Bad Wolf into Our Friend the Wolf.

The Wolf in both of these picture books insists that he has changed, that he has gotten stronger and more intelligent. He may be the Wolf, but he is not the same old Wolf who was duped, captured, or killed in the tales. The Wolf in the

---

[82]Ibid., 16; 17.
[83]Ibid., 30-31.

old tales attempted to disguise his true self and succeeded, at least momentarily, in overpowering and even making a meal of some of his victims. And while Pennart's improved Wolf still breaks into houses and disguises himself, he seems, however, to have lost some of his cunning along the way as evidenced by his letters to the papers. Instead of sneaking up on his *vieux amis*, the Wolf announces his return. And while initially the news stories seem to cause fear among the Pigs, Lamb, Goats, and Rabbit, they also give them time to flee. Like most of the endings of the various wolf tales to which the characters allude, Pennart's Wolf loses. The main difference, however, is not so much in the Wolf's behavior as in his victims' response: instead of killing him like in "The Goat and the Seven Kids," "The Three Little Pigs," and Grimm's version of "Little Red Riding Hood," or capturing him as in *Peter and the Wolf*, they offer him dinner in exchange for his promise of good behavior and scary wolf stories. In other words, the Wolf in Pennart's story is reformed, not killed by his folk and fairy tale victims.

The plot of *Le loup sentimental* is also built on a "fairy tale salad mix" of characters. Here, a young wolf named Lucas sets out to make his way in the world. Before leaving home, there are many tearful moments as he and his family say their good-byes. Aside from the folk tale premise of a child going out into the world, the conversations surrounding Lucas' parting are reminiscent of earlier versions of "Little Red Riding Hood," *Peter and the Wolf*, and the "Three Pigs." His grandmother tells him that he is the sunshine of her life ("Little Red Riding Hood") while his grandfather reprimands him for turning down his gift, saying that one should never disobey his grandfather (*Peter and the Wolf*), and his three younger brothers play a parting song (Disney's version of *The Three Little Pigs*).

From images of cows, pigs, and sheep to portraits of other wolves, Pennart fills Lucas' home with visual clues reflecting his lupine heritage and way of life. The watch given to him by his Grandfather alludes to the children's game, "What time is it Grandfather Wolf?" Further, Pennart's depiction of Lucas' father, especially his clothes, suggests that he is none other than the Wolf, *Le Loup*, of *Le loup est revenu!* and *Je suis revenu*. His father's gift to him, a list of things which are *bons à manger* or "good to eat," is perhaps the most obvious allusion to Lucas' heritage. On it appears the names of characters from various fairy and folk tales: Mother Goat and her seven kids, Little Red Riding Hood, the Three Pigs, Peter, and Tom Thumb and his brothers.

As Lucas walks along the path, he begins to get hungry. At that moment he sees coming towards him Mother Goat and her seven kids. Inquiring after their names, he announces that they are near the top of his list and he will eat them. Mother Goat insists, however, that if Lucas eats one, he must eat them all as it would be too painful for them to be separated. Mother Goat's response evokes the grief in her traditional tale as well as Lucas' mother's own pain at his parting. Moved, Lucas says he is not that hungry and lets them pass. The pattern repeats itself as he meets Little Red Riding Hood and the Three Pigs. With each new encounter he begins to drool, but as he hears their pleas the drool is replaced by tears. His final encounter is with a boy and his duck. By this time Lucas is very hungry. Seeing them he licks his lips and asks the boy who he is. Peter tells him his name, adding that in coming to hunt a wolf, he has disobeyed his grandfather. Lucas responds by shouting at him that one should never disobey their grandfather (« ON NE DESOBEIT JAMAIS A SON GRAND-PERE, TU M'ENTENDS ? »). These encounters foreground the ways in which Lucas and his potential victims are similar. The similarities even extend to Peter. As Lucas relinquishes his potential meals, he comments on his leniency and emotion, asking himself if one has ever seen such a sentimental wolf: « A-t-on déjà vu un loup aussi sentimental? ».[84]

Lucas eventually comes upon the house of an ogre. It is here that Lucas will finally be able to eat and where Lucas's actions will render him a hero. When the ogre insults Lucas and slams the door in his face, the good, kind wolf goes into a rage and breaks down the door.[85] It is only after having killed and eaten the giant, however, that Lucas becomes aware of a group of small boys locked in a cage. The presence of the small children makes it clear that Lucas, while stumbling across characters from traditional wolf tales, has stumbled into the story of Petit Poucet and his brothers. In killing the giant, Lucas inadvertently saved the little boy and his brothers.

Even though Lucas's list of good things to eat includes folk and fairy tale characters, it is clear from the start that Lucas is different from most European and Euro-American folk and fairy tale wolves. Unlike the wolf of "Little Red Riding Hood," "The Wolf and the Seven Kids," "The Three Little Pigs," or the wolf of Aesop's fables, Lucas is not a lone wolf. While he may be a young disperser wolf setting out to make his way in life, up until that moment he has been part of a family of wolves. Further, his family loves him and sends him out in the world with words of love and gifts. If the wolf in Western European folktales was a metaphor for human predation and gluttony, Pennart's Lucas is more akin to a young human leaving home to make his or her way in the world. The parting scene and his recollections of it as he makes his way through the woods bring to the fore that which is best and most treasured in human behavior and society: family, compassion, and sympathy. Pennart's illustrations of Lucas also point to a gentleness that folk and fairy tale wolves lack. In the family scenes at the beginning of the book, Lucas' smaller frame underscores his youth. And with youth comes not only an innocence but also ignorance as

---

[84]Pennart, Le loup sentimental (Paris : L'Ecole des loisirs, 1998), 27, 28.
[85]Ibid., 33-34.

suggested by the list that his father gives him. Even when Lucas kills, he kills a child-eating ogre. The wolf Lucas no longer threatens children or domesticated animals, but instead mirrors them.

Le loup, la chèvre, et les 7 chevreaux and Chapeau rond rouge derive their basic plot lines from their traditional counterparts. As such, they are more explicit examples of what Gerard Genette describes as hypertexts or texts derived from pre-existing texts. Genette identifies two types of hypertextuality: transformation and imitation. Genette defines transformation as "saying the same thing differently" [« dire la meme chose autrement »], while imitation is "saying something different in a similar manner" [« dire autre chose semblablement »].[86] Genette's transformation is similar to Rodari's notion of a "new key" where for instance, one tells the same story in a different time or place or from a different point of view.[87] Pennart introduces several new keys in his versions of Le loup, la chèvre et les sept chevreaux and Chapeau rond rouge. Aside from situating them in a more contemporary context, he also hints that his characters know the tales. Unlike the wolf in more traditional renditions of Le loup, la chevre, et les sept chevreaux, Pennart's wolf knows the routine. Instead of building his disguise based on the kid goats' responses to his various attempts to gain entrance into their home, Pennart's story begins with the wolf Igor buying the necessary items for his disguise as the Mother Goat. In this way, that story unfolds from the wolf's perspective. Similarly, Chapeau rond rouge's response to her mother's warning about wolves suggests that she too has heard it all before: "Yeah, yeah, I know, there is a wolf. Don't worry mom, I know the tune." [« Oui, oui, je sais, il y a le loup. Ne t'en fais pas Maman, je connais la musique. »].[88] And as in Le loup est revenu!, Je suis revenu, and Le loup sentimental, Pennart undoes the wolf's fate: he survives his encounters with both the Mother Goat and Chapeau rond rouge.

Like their traditional counterparts, however, identity is at the core Pennart's versions. But whereas identity, or rather mistaken identity, had dangerous consequences in the traditional versions of the tales, Pennart uses it to humorous advantage.

Those who have read Le loup sentimental will recognize Igor as Lucas' father. Igor also bears an uncanny resemblance to the Wolf in Le loup est revenu! and Je suis revenu. Like the Wolf of the latter two stories, Igor is self-satisfied. Pleased with himself and his plans, he heads for his car, promising himself that "this day will memorable." [« Cette journee sera memorable ! »]. Knowing the routine, Igor drives to town to make some purchases. Stopping at various stores, he buys flour, shoes, a dress, and perfume. With packages in

---

[86]Gerard Genette, Palimpsestes (Paris: Editions du Seuil, 1982), 16; 14-15.
[87]Rodari, The Grammar of Fantasy, 51-52.
[88]Pennart, Chapeau rond rouge (Paris: Kaléidoscope, 2004), 9.

tow, he drives out to the woods to alter his identity from male wolf to female goat. He completes his transformation with a puff of goat cheese fragrance [« un soupçon de *Fleur de Chavignol* »]. Pennart's illustrations, which emphasize the long snouts and lankiness of both the goat and wolf, render Igor's transformation into the Mother Goat believable. Igor, imitating the voice of Mother Goat, gains entrance to the house by telling the children to open the door because the wolf is in the woods. As soon as the door is open, Igor adds in his own booming voice: "AND NOW HE IS IN THE HOUSE!" [« ET MAINTENANT IL EST DANS LA MAISON ! »].[89]

The Jerry Lewis-in-drag quality of Igor's appearance combined with slapstick humor prevents Igor from ever being a serious threat. Too clever for his own good, Igor is tripped up by a broken heel and tight dress. He falls, hits his head, and knocks himself out. As he lies unconscious, one of the kids telephones Father Goat while the others run and hide. As Igor begins to regain consciousness, Father Goat, who is conspicuously absent in the traditional tellings of this tale, arrives home to deal with Igor. Mayhem and mistaken identity continue when Madame Broutchou returns just in time to see her husband pick up Igor. Believing that she has caught her husband with another female in his arms, Madame Broutchou demands to know what this woman is doing in his arms. Henri, surprised by his wife's return, drops Igor who hits his head yet another time. As Madame Broutchou continues to berate her husband, Igor flees. Humiliated, Igor returns home, never to speak of that "memorable day!"[90]

In *Chapeau rond rouge*, Pennart updates the best-known wolf tale of all: "Little Red Riding Hood." Here the identity of the wolf is also at stake. Unlike Igor's attempts to hide his wolfish self, it is the failure of Chapeau rond rouge and her grandmother to see the wolf for what he is that triggers a series of comical misadventures.

Chapeau rond rouge, so-named because of the red hat she always wears, is sent to bring her grandmother two cakes and some butter for her birthday. Knowing the routine, Chapeau rond rouge avoids the woods so as not to encounter wolves. Walking through the fields, she comes upon "a big grey dog asleep against a haystack" [« un grand chien gris endormi contre une meule de foin. »]. Chapeau rond rouge, unlike her more traditional counterpart, has a sense of humor. Like Little Boy Blue, she blows her horn. The wolf, "completely terrorized," jumps up in the air. In the exchange that follows, Pennart captures the visual confusion inherent in illustrations of wolves (is it a dog or a wolf?), as well as the tendency of some people to conflate dogs and wolves. The dog-wolf confusion also evokes the French word for the large dogs

---

[89]Pennart, *Le loup, la chevre et les 7 chevreaux* (Paris: Kaléidoscope, 2005), 7, 20, 25.
[90]Ibid., 31, 36.

bred to hunt wolves: the *chien-loup* or wolfhound. Chapeau rond rouge, who gets a good laugh out of her victim's reaction, addresses him as a "dog," and offers him one of her cakes as a way to apologize for disturbing him. Recovering from such a hard and rude awakening, the wolf, unlike his traditional counterpart, makes no attempts at concealing his wolfish nature and instead corrects her: "I...I...I am not a dog, I...I...I am the wolf and I...I...I..." (« Je...je...je ne suis pas un chien, je...je...je suis le loup et je...je...je... »). Chapeau rond rouge, pointing at him, laughs at the notion of him being a wolf: "But no, you are not a wolf; the wolf lives in the forest and is very bad. You should see yourself, you, with your big gentle doggie face. [« Mais non, tu n'es pas le loup ; le loup vit dans la foret et il est très méchant. Tu t'es vu, toi, avec ta bonne bouille de toutou gentil ? »]. The more he insists that he is a wolf and not a dog, the more Chapeau rond rouge insists that he must be dreaming. As she leaves, in words that echo the traditional tellings, she discloses to the wolf where she is headed and why she must take the long route. "My grandmother is expecting me, I must go. You see the smoke, it's just over there, but on account of the wolf, I have to go around the forest. Good-bye my big dog..."[« ... Mère-Grand m'attend, faut que j'y aille. Tu vois la fumée, c'est juste la, mais a cause du loup, je dois contourner la foret. Au revoir mon gros chien... »].[91] After she departs, the wolf, talking to himself, promises that he will show her and takes off through the forest.

But alas, Pennart's retelling, situated in a contemporary context, has contemporary perils: crossing the road, the wolf is struck by a car, driven by none other than Chapeau rond rouge's grandmother. Like her granddaughter, she believes the wolf to be a dog. Relieved that he is not dead, she takes him home with her and puts him in her bed while she goes in search of a doctor.

The next two illustrations depicting Chapeau rond rouge's arrival recall traditional illustrations of the tale. We see the wolf in bed as she enters the house. Seeing her "grandmother" in bed, Chapeau rond rouge thinks that she looks bad and must be ill. Unlike her fairy tale counterpart, Pennart's heroine realizes her mistake: "But no! It is the big dog who plays at being a wolf." [« Mais non ! C'est ce gros chien qui joue au loup. »].[92] This last bit of text, *joue au loup*, alludes not only to her belief that the "dog" is pretending to be a wolf, but also to the children's game: *jouer au loup*, or to play wolf. Chapeau rond rouge's accusation that the sleeping canine has eaten her grandmother recalls the wolf behavior in the traditional tales. Once again, however, Chapeau rond rouge breaks with her traditional role. Believing her grandmother is dead, Chapeau rond rouge takes action to save her. After hitting the "dog" on the head with a candlestick, she opens his mouth to speak to her grandmother.

---

[91]Pennart, *Chapeau rond rouge*, 10, 13, 14-15, 16.
[92]Ibid., 26.

Promising to get her out of there, Chapeau rond rouge goes into the kitchen in search of a knife. This of course is the tried and true Grimms' tactic for excising the wolf's prey from his belly: slit open the abdomen and out pops the meal, healthy and whole, perhaps a little discombobulated.

In the knick of time, the grandmother returns with the doctor. Seeing the wolf on his back with his mouth open, looking worse than before, the grandmother fears he is dead. When Chapeau rond rouge hears her grandmother, she is relieved to see that her grandmother is alive but fears that she has killed the "dog." At this point the doctor steps in not only to reassure them that the animal will live, but to inform them that the animal in the bed is not a dog, but an "enormous wolf."[93] The wolf convalesces at the grandmother's house, where the grandmother nurses him back to health with medicine and steaks.

In the end Chapeau rond rouge grows up to be an internationally renowned wild animal doctor, while the wolf spends the rest of his days at her grandmother's side. We last see him sitting in front of the fire with the grandmother, helping her roll the yarn for her knitting. As Pennart explains, the wolf, "had to resign himself to his fate: his reputation as a ferocious wolf had taken a blow" [« il dut se résigner a son sort : sa réputation de loup féroce en avait pris un coup. »].[94]   And the blow had come from two humans: a small girl in a red hat and her grandmother.

Pennart's series of picture books featuring wolves recasts traditional characters in new roles while creating a lupine world. Through humor and allusion, Pennart's stories offer us wolves who *mirror* rather than *threaten* their traditional folk and fairy tale victims. No longer a metaphor for evil, the dangerous nature of the wolf, along with the cautionary nature of the tales, has disappeared. Whether overpowered by fellow characters or tripped up by contemporary modes of living, these wolves are benign and likeable. As such they reflect the stature of real wolves in the post-modern world.

---

[93]Ibid., 33.
[94]Ibid., 34.

CHAPTER FIVE

ONCE UPON A TIME IN IDAHO: TRANSFORMING CINDERELLA THROUGH A-TEMPORALITY, AWKWARDNESS, AND ADOLESCENCE IN *NAPOLEON DYNAMITE*[95]

LANCE WELDY

[*Editor's note*: The material in this article was originally presented at a panel for the 33rd annual conference of the Children's Literature Association at Manhattan Beach, California, in 2006. The contents of this article are the genesis of a potential full-length study on *Napoleon Dynamite* and will therefore only touch broadly on the topic at this specific time.]

I. Introduction to *Napoleon*

I think there is nothing wrong with attaching yourself to certain projects simply because you like the material. Just this summer in my graduate class, I discussed the major paper assignment and advised my students to find a book and topic that they have a personal interest in. The underlying precept behind this advice was that if they will be devoting an extended amount of time and energy on a project, it might as well be on something with which they have some pleasurable connection. This mentality is how I came upon this project and this thesis about the film, *Napoleon Dynamite*.[96] Unlike other viewers who either *consistently* hated this film or have grown to love this film over a series of

---

[95]This essay would not have been possible without Kate Pyle, a high school classmate of mine, who knew this film was my kind of humor and recommended it to me. She came over to my house on the holidays and introduced me to this film on DVD. Incidentally, she actually gave me her copy of the DVD under the condition that I "pay it forward" and buy a copy for someone else, which I did for my brother and his family, and they were instantly hooked! This very form of advertising—word of mouth—would be a fascinating research topic, especially concerning this unique Independent film.

[96]*Napoleon Dynamite*, dir. John Hess, 82 min., Fox, 2004, DVD.

viewings, I immediately found myself drawn to this film and its unique humor, but I wasn't exactly sure why. I couldn't place my finger on the attraction I felt towards this text. I kept asking myself, "Why was this film more than just a popular movie with one-liners that my students love to quote?"

Before I discuss my rhetorical attraction, let me tell you how a few others have found this film rhetorically appealing. Andres Pinter's aptly titled magazine article in *Rolling Stone*, "The Reign of Napoleon," gives great insight into this rhetorical analysis:

> In early April, Idaho State Rep. Larry C. Bradford stood before the Legislature to present Resolution No. 29, honoring the state's most significant cultural contribution in memory. "Be it resolved by the Legislature of the State of Idaho," he began, launching into the twenty-point bill: "Whereas Tater Tots figure prominently in this film thus promoting Idaho's most famous export. . . Whereas Kip's relationship with LaFawnduh is a tribute to e-commerce and Idaho's technology-driven industry. . ." Bradford concluded by declaring any members who vote "nay" to be "FREAKIN' IDIOTS!" Resolution No. 29, paying tribute to *Napoleon Dynamite*, passed unanimously.[97]

I'd like to point out that this document that Pinter quotes brings to mind at least two positive political attractions for Idaho, both dealing with commerce and trade: potatoes and technology (internet). Indeed, this film has hit pop culture status and contributed, as Bradford says, "significant cultural contribution."

Furthermore, Pinter asks himself the similar question I had been pondering when he says, "How did this quirkiest, produced by a group of Mormons, make the leap to pop-culture phenomenon?" While his article doesn't completely answer this question, it does provide a few ideas, the most notable one referring to the universality aspect of the film. Pinter refers to Nikki Sixx of the band Motley Crüe who says, "There's a little bit of Napoleon in all of us." But, as I referred to briefly earlier, this film brings out unpredictable responses from different people. Its absurdist nature may elicit laughs, or sneers, of bewilderment. Ironically, the universality of this film can be found from the fans' individual attraction. As the film's lead, John Heder, says in Pinter's article, "There's a million people who think they're the only ones who get it." [98] In other words, the low-budget, off-key nature hits a positive nerve with many people who believe that a film finally sees the perceived individual quirkiness in all of us.

Immediately after my first viewing, I knew I wanted to incorporate this text into my academic repertoire, but I wasn't quite sure how or for what purpose. And I believe this gestation period was the fun, mentally challenging time where

---

[97]Andres Pinter, "The Reign of Napoleon," *Rolling Stone*, 2 June 2005, 31.
[98]Ibid.

I spent weeks and months mulling over various scenes and conversations I had with other enthusiasts of this film. Part of the academic inquiry involved when we approach a project is asking ourselves, "What is this text's rhetorical attraction?" (In other words, "Why do I like this film?" or "What about this film do I find so touching that I want to write about it?") The immediate, obvious response for this film for me was that most of us enjoy viewing films about adolescence, but not necessarily because we enjoyed it ourselves. On the contrary, we more than likely hated at least some aspect of this awkward phase and are glad we don't have to go through it again. Yet, there is this somewhat sadistic side to us that finds it more than satisfactory to vicariously experience adolescence through someone else on-screen. And we might even delight in the fact that, even though we believe we suffered egregiously, someone out there had it even worse than we.

And that's where this film comes into play. Napoleon Dynamite represents an extremely naïve, sometimes-lovable nerd in the TV tradition of Steve Urkel from *Family Matters* and Samuel "Screech" Powers from *Saved by the Bell*. But my attraction to this film doesn't stop there; I felt there was something more. This was such an odd film, produced on an extremely low budget, and incorporating seemingly absurd elements through dialogue and cultural artifacts from many different decades, that I knew there was something more to this film than just a comedic, independent film about high school. It was then I looked at this film through the lens of a fairy tale structure. At the time I was teaching fairy tales to undergraduates, so I had studied the nature of folk tales quite a bit. I realized I had found a way to explain the attraction of this film's surreal, absurd nature in a way that encapsulates issues of adolescence, and because I have been writing about transformation in various formats in my academic career, I knew this project of a fairy-tale adaptation for contemporary audiences would work.

Napoleon Dynamite, a 2004 Independent Film, has reached cult classic status in just a short amount of time, especially with today's college students. I would argue that one reason for *Dynamite*'s success rests in the film's positive portrayal of an updated Cinderella figure while providing universally recognized high school situations. However, instead of enacting teen angst in a *Breakfast Club*-like setting, director Jared Hess successfully uses Time to serve as more than a backdrop to show how complex and challenging the transitional stage of adolescence can be. *Napoleon Dynamite* draws together the topics of Time, Adolescence, and Fairy Tales into film perfectly. Essentially, Napoleon serves as an anti-hero in an unconventional fairy tale where the protagonist does not undergo a magical, beautifying transformation, and where Time functions as an a-temporal, decade-synchronous factor in conjunction with a rural, almost unnamed, setting to give the audience an atypical Hollywood Fairy Tale film.

As Jennifer Vadeboncoeur states in *Re/Constructing "the Adolescent,"* "Bakhtin notes that the construction of the self is a social process, a reflection of self and other relationships, and as such it is fraught with both tensions and comforts. [. . .] Our own perception of achieving selfhood is a timeless, incomplete, and contextually bound process.   Indeed, we are always *becoming.*"[99]   In other words, Time for the adolescent becomes somewhat frozen, a-temporal, as he or she conceives his or her identity. Also in this same vein, Irwin Lieb states in *Past, Present, and Future*, "The past is continuous with what is present, and it affects it just as what is passing does, not by acting on it but just by being past, by being the time and being in which activity ends."[100]   Throughout the film, Hess infuses cultural artifacts from the 1970s, 80s, and 90s into a present-day setting. By integrating and assigning past decades to Napoleon and his circle of friends and family, Hess has illustrated how Napoleon fits into the Cinderella-like lower circles of the social status structure. For Napoleon, Time shows his inability to socialize through a visible delineation between his penchant for the 1980/90s and the "normal" present-day popular students.

One of the biggest names in fairy tale scholarship is Jack Zipes, and I will be looking at two of his works extensively during this study. Zipes' *Happily Ever After* analyzes how films have adapted fairy tales: "The fairy tale has [. . .] also been changed in innovative ways to instill hope in its youthful and mature audiences so that no matter how bad their lives are, they can still believe that they can live happily ever after."[101]   Modern audiences of all social status can appreciate Napoleon, the Cinderella figure, who manages to successfully accomplish his fairy tale quest in an unlikely manner. Blurring the time by incorporating elements of the past three decades supports this "once upon a time" fairy tale setting of *Napoleon Dynamite.*

As stated in the editor's note, some time in the future I plan on expanding this original essay into an extended monograph, but for the purposes of this essay, I first want to establish how *Napoleon Dynamite* qualifies as a fairy tale before showing how this film conveys a transformed, postmodern Cinderella figure through an unconventional use of Time and Fairy Tales, thereby

---

[99]Jennifer Vadeboncoeur, "'I'm Acting It out Here and Now': Analyzing Chronotopes in Institutional Contexts and Identity Narratives," in *Re/Constructing "the Adolescent": Sign, Symbol and Body*, ed. Jennifer Vadeboncoeur and Lisa Patel Stevens (New York: Peter Lang, 2005), 127.

[100] Irwin Lieb, *Past, Present, and Future: A Philosophical Essay about Time* (Urbana, IL: University of Illinois Press, 1991), 162.

[101]Jack Zipes, *Happily Ever After: Fairy Tales, Children, and the Culture Industry* (New York: Routledge, 1997), 6.

depicting awkward Adolescence through its portrayal of fashion, music, and technology.

Because I realize that, even though this film has hit pop culture phenomenon status, not everyone has seen or heard much about this film, I wanted to briefly provide a summary of the film before commencing. The very absurd nature of this film makes any plot summarizing difficult and would in fact be an interesting study as to how different people might summarize this elusive film. However, I believe I have found a great, succinct summary from Jennifer Grzeskowiak's article. She says,

> For the uninitiated, the low-budget film follows Napoleon Dynamite, a socially awkward teenager who enjoys milk tasting and drawing mythical creatures, through his adventures at high school and home, which include helping his best friend Pedro, a recent Mexican immigrant, win the election for student body president. All the while he must deal with his idiosyncratic family members, such as his online-dating-obsessed brother and Tupperware-selling uncle.[102]

II. Fairy Tales Elements and *Napoleon*

First, I want to show how this film exhibits fairy tale elements before applying specific Cinderella qualities. It's quite obvious that Hollywood loves to capitalize on a financially good thing, and literary adaptations have long been a popular, commercially-successful endeavor. (Classic novels by authors like Charles Dickens and Jane Austen have enjoyed adaptation after adaptation. And Sara Crabtree's article touches on one of the very successful *Harry Potter* adaptations.) Plus, the mythical landscape of Hollywood could arguably serve as a means by which someone may actualize the American Dream. Zipes actually devotes a book to the idea of fairy tales and culture in *Happily Ever After*. He says that "Hollywood as a symbol is a utopian fairy-tale destination, a place where the good fairy as destiny waits to transform unknown talents into known stars, where fortunes are made, where, like the enchanted forest, something special happens that brings genuine happiness to the true in heart."[103] Few statements could be more applicable to John Heder's life than this one. It's almost as though the making of this movie was taken from a fairy tale blueprint. The film was made on a student's budget and produced independently. It played at the Sundance Film Festival and was acquired for a modest sum by Fox. Heder, who plays Napoleon, was cast because he was a one-time roommate of the director, and he was only paid $1,000.00 for his part. As the

---

[102]Jennifer Grzeskowiak, "Celebrating Celebrity: Preston, Idaho, Hosts First Annual *Napoleon Dynamite* Festival," *American City and County*, August 2005, 65.
[103]Zipes, *Happily Ever After*, 2.

film's popularity hit the mainstream theater and DVD audiences, Heder morphed from an unknown to the man everyone wanted to cast. Since the phenomenal success of this movie, Heder has been given roles in several high profile movies. His career is the epitome of the American Dream, and the American society at large admires and appreciates stories such as his.

So why discuss the fairy-tale elements of this movie? Well, as Zipes notes, "Even more appealing to children are fairy-tale films, which take precedence over literature. I do not mean that children do not read fairy tales anymore or have tales read to them. Rather, children are more readily exposed to fairy-tale films through television and movie theaters than through books."[104] One needn't think hard to list a few popular fairy tale movies (including and excluding Disney). Though the format or characters may be transformed, the fairy tale elements remain the same, which is why I believe *Napoleon Dynamite*, though an updated fairy tale, finds a loyal audience. In fact, *Napoleon Dynamite* represents that kind of unique fairy-tale movie Zipes refers to when he says "in order for the viewer to determine whether there is something new, meaningful, and utopian in the fairy-tale film, he or she must know the origins of the story."[105] While his statement refers to children's inability to distinguish between Hollywood updates and original fairy tales, I believe few adults would be able to discuss how *Napoleon* differs from, say, Grimm's "Aschenputtel." Nevertheless, I will spend the second main portion of this essay showing how *Napoleon* provides a new and meaningful postmodern Cinderella story.

To assist in conveying my two main points, I am including two appendices in the form of spreadsheets, one spreadsheet per main point. Appendix A covers the characteristics of a fairy tale and how *Napoleon* factors into as well as strays from (in a postmodern vein) these elements. Likewise, Appendix B looks at Donna Norton's basic schematics for the Cinderella story and how *Napoleon* updates these elements. Basically, even children can identify a fairy tale they are either watching or reading through these three main elements. The first, **Setting**, is usually the dead giveaway right from the beginning with those famous words, "Once upon a time, a long time ago, in a land far away." With these fairy tales like "Sleeping Beauty" and "Snow White," we are never given a specific place or time. Likewise, it is rare if we are ever given famous landmarks or indicators of a specific decade. What this vagueness does is provide universality for the tales, something that all readers can appreciate and follow. For *Napoleon Dynamite*, we have that same sense of vagueness in terms of place and time that, I would argue, provides the viewing audience with the feeling that this story could happen in many different communities and not one specific place. Throughout the film, we see different settings such as different

---

[104]Ibid., 10.
[105]Ibid., 72-73.

residential houses: a medium-sized family house (the Dynamites'), a suburban housing community (Uncle Rico's sales route), an upper-class house (Summer Wheatley's), and an immigrant house (Pedro's). As most adolescent novels and films do, this film spends an ample amount of time covering what most would experience at the high school: cafeteria (the famous Tater Tots scene), the classroom (the Happy Hands Club scene), the gymnasium (the Dance scene), the hallways (the "Vote for Pedro" decorating scene), the playground (the Tether Ball scene), the track (the Physical Education scene), and the auditorium (the Class President Speeches scene).

But besides the universal domestic and school settings, the geographic setting provides the viewer with a somewhat perplexing task of pinpointing a place that contains all of the following: rolling plains, giant hills, sparsely populated country, a public telephone in the middle of nowhere, a small downtown shopping community, and sand dunes. It is interesting that Hess has subtly let the audience know that this film indeed was shot locally in southern Idaho, but only the keen viewer will notice this. Only rarely does the story provide this information: the only two major clues come in dialogue and a commercial sign. First, the principal disciplines Pedro for making a piñata in the form of his rival, Summer Wheatley. The principal tells Pedro he is not sure how things are done in Juarez, but "here in Idaho we have something called pride. Understand? Smashing in the face of a piñata that resembles Summer Wheatley is a disgrace to you, me, and the entire Gem State." Also, behind the principal is an object that looks like a football trophy in the form of the state of Idaho.

The only other obvious hint comes whenever Kip is at the bus station waiting for LaFawnduh. The sign behind him says, "IDAGO BUS LINES" in huge letters, surrounded by information that lets us know it was established in 1946 and that it's the Preston, Idaho, bus station. Also, on the windows are the words, "Scenic Idaho," but even with all this information, without being able to pause the DVD, a viewer may not be able to catch it all. Other than these two clues, the viewer would have to do research to find out that this film was shot on location in Idaho using a majority of the locals as the actors.

One could very well point out that this film is not truly universal because it does not include a bustling metropolitan city, but while some people may never live the small town life, Dean L. May notes, "The simple fact is that both Native American and European societies in North America, since their earliest plantation, have been overwhelmingly rural and agrarian. Not until 1920 did the number of urban dwellers in the United States begin to surpass the number of rural dwellers."[106] What May's quotation means is that notwithstanding the last

---

[106]May, Dean L May, *Three Frontiers: Family, Land, and Society in the American West, 1850-1900*, (Cambridge: Cambridge University Press, 1994) 1-2.

approximately 80 years, the universal experience, at least as far as the American experience is concerned, has been predominantly rural.

But this vagueness of setting goes beyond place. Arguably more important for this film's sense of vagueness for fairy tale elements is the issue of time. As many viewers will have noticed, this movie blends and blurs time with the help of cultural artifacts, such as fashion, music, and technology. One way to catalogue the differences in time would be to focus on which characters are wearing which kinds of clothes. Noticeably, Napoleon and his world of friends and family wear fashion trends at least a decade behind what the "normal" popular kids are wearing. Another way of cataloguing this film's use of time is by listing cultural artifacts from each decade: because of my limited time and space, I will only mention a few representative artifacts. Naturally, it is difficult to pinpoint exactly which decade some artifacts come from because fashion styles reach different parts of the United States at different times.

As far as the 1970s go, Uncle Rico serves as the definitive representative character. Everything from his van to his clothes and hair screams the '70s. Plus, it is Rico who constantly wishes to go back to his high school days of 1982 where he could change time and become a successful football star. Uncle Rico's desire to return to the past consumes him so much that he makes a fool of himself and looks for a savior in technology. Unfortunately for him (and for Napoleon), Rico's online purchase of a time machine is in actuality an electrocutor. One other noticeable cultural artifact from the '70s is not really from the '70s at all, which reinforces the postmodern tone. The most famous scene of the film, Napoleon's dance in the auditorium, is accompanied by the song "Canned Heat" by Jamiroquai. While the song sounds like a '70s disco number, it is, in actuality, a retro disco number sung by a contemporary artist.

If Uncle Rico represents the '70s, Napoleon and his world represent the '80s. Napoleon's wardrobe definitely screams 1980s, with his T-shirt wardrobe, parachute pants with the side zipper, the famous pair of moon boots, and his large glasses that cover most of his face. Also noticeably '80s in terms of fashion is Napoleon's friend Deb, who consistently wears the side pony tail, stretch pants with matching belt, and an overabundant amount of bracelets. Napoleon relies on '80s technology when he watches the instructional dance video tape; the VCR requires him to insert the tape into the compartment that opens at the top of the machine. And finally, two pieces of music represent the '80s. First, the quintessential '80s slow-dance song, "Time after Time" by Cyndi Lauper, plays at the high school dance, and last is the final song we hear as Napoleon and Deb play tether ball, the '80s song, "The Promise" by the group When in Rome.

Cultural artifacts from the '90s can be found in both technology and music. First, while Uncle Rico may dress and act like he's still living in the '70s, he uses a '90s-looking camcorder to record his football tosses. In his opening scene, which comes after Napoleon's grandmother suffers an injury, Uncle Rico is called on his '90s-looking cellular phone to help out at the Dynamite house. As far as 90's music is concerned, it is interesting that Summer, the popular girl, dances to the Backstreet Boys' song, "Larger than Life," because the song debuted around 1999. While most teens generally stray from being attached to recently outdated songs, it makes sense that Summer's popular group dances to a song that is at least closer to contemporary times.

Summer's group definitely serves as the contemporary looking group of this film in terms of dress and demeanor, yet it is fascinating that her group is not the only one using contemporary artifacts. While Uncle Rico may be using 90's technology, Napoleon's brother Kip spends his time chatting on the internet with LaFawnduh, a pastime we generally associate with the early part of the 21st century.

The second basic element of a fairy tale, the **plot**, is also clearly recognizable for children. First, the story can be boiled down to a conflict between good and evil, where the two sides are *clearly* demarcated. This category may be a little tricky when applying it to *Napoleon*, however, because it supports the film's contemporary, postmodern perspective and asks the question, "Who is good and who is evil in this film?" Definitely we are sympathetic towards Napoleon because he is the protagonist; the tale is told mainly through his perspective. Consequently, we are practically forced to hate Summer and her gang for no other reason than that they are popular, good-looking, and stuck-up. But just how "good" is Napoleon? From the very beginning of the film, we are introduced to Napoleon's erratic, explosive behavior through the dialogue he shares with a young boy on the school bus. When the boy innocently asks Napoleon what he is going to do today, Napoleon replies, "Whatever I feel like I want to do. GOSH!" This is not an innocent Prince Charming, but rather a realistic classmate with a chip on his shoulder, the kind of student that perhaps many of us remember having from our own high school days.

It's obvious that a recent, popular movie will not have much academic scholarship written about it yet, which is all the more reason for *Napoleon* aficionados to offer their "skills" and contribute. For example, an in-depth character analysis of Napoleon is warranted. After I presented a form of this paper at the ChLA, we had an interesting discussion about how we as an audience feel about Napoleon. Do we feel sorry for Napoleon because he is getting picked on? Or does he deserve being bullied for his caustic attitude and making up fantastic stories? And in what direction are we laughing—*at* or *with* Napoleon? These are just a few questions that need in-depth answers. And just briefly, I need to comment on Uncle Rico's character. From the moment we are introduced to his character, we realize he is shady, but it's not until halfway through the movie we realize just how creepy he is. In terms of our good and evil category, Uncle Rico could serve as a secondary villain.

Before I move to the last of the three basic fairy tale elements, I will add one more thing about plot. Fairy tales have happy endings. Typically, a fairy tale will end with a marriage, and children can recite the usual ending phrase of a tale: "and they all lived happily ever after." Likewise, Napoleon experiences a happy ending, not by marriage, but by public approval from his peers, after which we see a montage of happy endings for Kip and LaFawnduh, Grandma and Tina, Uncle Rico and his girlfriend, Pedro and his family (showing one of the few times that Pedro ever smiles), and finally, Napoleon and Deb. Incidentally, Chapter 19 on the DVD is titled "Happy Endings," and the DVD includes an added epilogue of a wedding between Kip and LaFawnduh.

The last basic fairy tale element exhibited in *Napoleon* is the use of **characters**. Discussing the complexities of the character reveals how Napoleon twists the traditional fairy tale. Typically in fairy tales, the characters are universal—simple, flat, almost stock characters. This type of character is not coincidental when considering that the kind of basic plot required of the traditional fairy tale needs a flat good character against a flat evil character. While Napoleon is simple and flat, he is also universal. As the earlier quotations from *Rolling Stone* signify, we can see the nerd in us through him, and if not the nerd in us, at least the nerds we knew about from personal experiences. (This also was a topic of conversational interest at the paper presentation, which boiled down to the question: "Are you a Napoleon or a Summer?") Nevertheless, it is at this point where we see the postmodern side of the tale coming through. Napoleon is an antihero, and his name is anything but generic like a Jack or Hansel. If anything, his name alludes to a specific type of behavior and mindset.

Furthermore, as Appendix A shows, not only are fairy tale protagonists flat, but they are also static, which means they seldom undergo a significant internal change. You don't see Rapunzel changing her ways at the end of the story, nor would you see Snow White making the realization that she was wrong about the wicked queen. In this sense, Napoleon follows the fairy tale format because he doesn't really undergo any internal or external change. His same apathetic demeanor can be found from beginning to end, including the listless eyes and hunched-over posture. In a fascinating, postmodern twist, the change comes outside of the protagonist. At the climax (the Student President Speeches), Napoleon makes the audience come to him in the famous dance sequence which epitomizes the bizarre uniqueness that is Napoleon. He doesn't change himself for the audience, but instead makes the audience come to him. His last line of the movie, "Wanna play me?" is indicative of just how static Napoleon is, for it's the same tether ball request from the middle of the movie that Napoleon gives to Summer. Of course, this time, Deb, the proper mate for Napoleon, responds affirmatively.

III. Cinderella Motifs—with *Napoleon*

The phenomenon of Cinderella is not new, and the purpose of this essay is not to cover the history of Cinderella as other, more competent scholars have done. Instead, I want to briefly provide what some academic scholars have said about Cinderella in particular, and fairy tales in general, before showing how Napoleon serves as an updated, postmodern Cinderella model.

Arguably the most popular fairy tale, the very name "Cinderella" has been attached to several recent high profile Hollywood films like *A Cinderella Story* and *Cinderella Man*, which again supports just how amenable the Cinderella variant can be to transformations. Scholars too have looked at the influence of Cinderella. For instance, Huang Mei's work actually looks at the "transformation of the Cinderella theme in the works of English novelists."[107] Huang says, "I would like to suggest that the mutations and vicissitudes the Cinderella theme has undergone are in one way or another connected to the 'actual' life and to the consciousness of the people of the time."[108] What Mei's statement contributes to this essay is the reality of adolescence, and how intricate this reality, with all its awkwardness, ties in to a fairy tale story. In other words, *Napoleon Dynamite* is the reflection of, in Mei's words, the "consciousness of the people of the time" by casting an irritable, yet somehow loveable, adolescent antihero in the role of Cinderella who manages not only to save the story and contribute to the Happy Ending, but also to do so with his awkward "skills." This kind of transformation is certainly telling of postmodern times.

In *Breaking the Magic Spell: Radical Theories of Folk and Fairy Tales*, Jack Zipes devotes a chapter to Mass Media and Culture, specifically with how fairy tales have been translated into film. He says that

> The reception of folk and fairy tales in the Western world [. . .] has been heavily influenced by the Walt Disney industry and other similar corporations so that most people have preconceived notions of what a fairy tale is and should be. The media rely on our preformed imaginations to suggest in every manner and form that Disney-like utopias are ones which we should all strive to construct in

---

[107]Mei, Huang, *Transforming the Cinderella Dream: From Frances Burney to Charlotte Brontë* (New Brunswick, NJ: Rutgers University Press, 1990), ix.
[108]Ibid., x.

reality, and, if that were not enough, we even have concrete Disneylands as blueprints for our imagination to show that they can be constructed.[109]

What amazes me is how far Disney has further perpetuated this blueprint since this 1979 passage. As Zipes so eloquently notes, the imagination of the public thinks of fairy tales in terms of Disney movies. It is always fascinating to teach "Aschenputtel" to my undergraduates because for them, Grimm is not the standard litmus test by which other tales should be compared, but rather the 1950 Disney film version. Consequently, the majority of them are aghast at the ending of Grimm's story, which is so un-Disney. But Zipes doesn't stop there. He also says,

> To counter this corporate inundation of our imagination, the familiar fairy tales must be made strange to us again if we are to respond to unique images of our own imagination and the possible utopian elements they may contain. Otherwise the programmed fairy-tale images will continue to warp our sensibilities in TV advertisements such as the ones which have women transformed into Cinderellas by magically buying new dresses, paying money for beauty treatments in a health spa, using the proper beautifying cosmetics.[110]

What *Napoleon Dynamite* does so well is to provide what Zipes calls for in an alternate, unique way of looking at the Cinderella fairy tale. Sure, there are a few male Cinderella figures already in literary and pop culture history, but including a male Cinderella is just the beginning of how this film deviates from the stereotypical blueprint. As a holistic whole, this film makes the whole Cinderella concept strange again by popularizing a deluded, absurdist antihero who is one Cinderella figure not magically transformed into a beautiful creature. Napoleon has no godmother and no make-over, yet he still manages to overcome the adversity an average (or even less-than-average) adolescent faces on a daily basis. Two other times Zipes discusses the issue of making meaning out of plot and storytelling. First, he says, "To write about the historical transformations of the fairy tale means writing about struggles over voice, storytelling, and the socialization of children."[111] Next, he says that all fairy tales were "structured similarly to promise happiness if one could 'properly' read their plots and symbols, even when tragedy occurred."[112] Both of these statements connect to the postmodern essence of *Napoleon Dynamite*. This film is hardly a predictable movie partly because the plot isn't really discernible until

---

[109]Jack Zipes, *Breaking the Magic Spell: Radical Theories of Folk and Fairy Tales,* (Austin, TX: University of Texas Press, 1979), 105.
[110]Ibid.
[111]Zipes, *Happily Ever After*, 3.
[112]Ibid., 4.

at least half-way through the film.   Furthermore, the very narratological structure of this film depicts an adolescent world filled with awkward scenes, dialogue, and action.

To better appreciate the postmodern elements this fairy tale transformation brings, I am providing Appendix B, which shows eight categories created by Donna Norton.[113]   These categories are not meant to be exhaustive by any stretch of the imagination.   Out of the extant hundreds to thousands of Cinderella variants, very few could fit all eight of Norton categories.   That being said, I believe her categories provide academic studies a great blueprint when trying to find commonalities of the Cinderella tale.   The appendix shows Norton's example of plugging Cinderella into her eight categories with the two most famous variants from Perrault and Brothers Grimm. (Her original chart contains variants from other different cultures as well.) I believe these two stories can provide an interesting contrast to Napoleon, which is why I included them.   In the time and space I have left, I want to highlight briefly how Napoleon fits or responds to the majority of these categories while occasionally mentioning Grimm's or Perrault's for sake of contrast.

The first category, **Cause of Lowly Position**, is somewhat of a mystery and brings up sociological and behavioral questions.   In the popular variants, the death of the mother is the easily identifiable reason for Cinderella's low status. However, the reason for Napoleon's sub-status is not given at the beginning of the story.   What we do know is that his parents are missing (another common fairy tale motif) and that his guardian, his grandmother, doesn't impart the best social interaction skills.   For example, at one point, Napoleon whines about what to eat while grandmother is away.   In a huff, she yells that he can heat up a "dang quesadilla."   In her defense, perhaps her patience has worn thin as it appears she has been the guardian of this child for quite some time.   Her no-nonsense reaction to Napoleon's childish behavior raises the big question for this category: "Why is Napoleon's attitude the way it is?"   In other words, is his nerdy appearance the cause of his caustic attitude which serves as some sort of defense mechanism? Or is it his caustic attitude that has caused him to look and act the way he does, which therefore gives him a lowly position both in school and at home?

Outward Signs of Lowly Position is the second category, and we see some noticeable signs of lowly Napoleon being pitted against Uncle Rico and Kip. Like in Perrault's version of Cinderella where the younger step-sister is kind to Cinderella, so is Kip kinder to Napoleon than Uncle Rico.   Nevertheless, as the youngest, he is humiliated and ridiculed into feeding Tina, the family llama, because Napoleon is the only one who doesn't have a job.   To make matters

---

[113]Donna Norton, *Through the Eyes of a Child*, 4th ed. (Englewood Cliffs, N.J: Merrill, 1995), 316.

worse, Napoleon attempts to make money by performing demeaning tasks at a chicken farm, ultimately to discover he had only been making slave wages. The third category, **Relationship to Household**, loosely connects to the first two. Napoleon is considered a child and a baby who doesn't have a job.

The next category, **How He Receives Wishes**, is a good example of how this postmodern transformation deviates from the traditional tale. As I mentioned before, Napoleon never undergoes a magical transformation and therefore never receives wishes by a fairy godmother that children and adults naturally associate with Disney fairy tales. It is significant that, as an anti-hero, he enacts his own agency. If we consider the school dance as equivalent to the traditional royal ball, we can observe how Napoleon draws a picture of Trisha and gives it to her, an endearing act that deserves, according to Trisha's mom, a date to the dance. Yes, in a small sense he is rescued from being stranded by a godmother-like character through Pedro's relatives, but ultimately, his ticket to the dance is all his own. Unfortunately, Napoleon is humiliated by Trisha at the dance when she ditches him for Summer's group.

What Keeps Him from Social Occasion is another example of a postmodern category because there are two different kinds of social occasions. The first one, the dance, is unsuccessful for Napoleon. Not only is Napoleon left stranded in the middle of nowhere as Uncle Rico tries to sell Tupperware, but he is also publicly humiliated by Trisha at the dance. However, the second occasion—the Student Body speeches—really serves as the springboard for Napoleon's success as an anti-hero. He uses his unique character qualities to win over the student body with his unusual dance routine. Another important postmodern point to note here is that, although Napoleon is the protagonist of the film and the antihero, his action is not intended to glorify himself, but instead to support Pedro for President. Throughout their friendship in the film, Napoleon only desires to serve as Pedro's sidekick, a veritable Sancho Panza. In his efforts, Napoleon actually wows not a prince or princess, but the whole audience, all in attendance. Even his dance, though perhaps out of character, remains within the realm of his own weirdness, exhibiting a comedic incongruity between a nerdy white boy and the urban-esque moves he imitates from a video by D-Quon.

What makes this scene significantly unique yet at the same time traditional is the classic Napoleonic comment of encouragement wrapped up in a naively haughty, yet comedic tone of puffed-up grandeur: a comment that arguably serves as the moral to this tale. Zipes mentions that "the Grimms purposely changed their fairy tales between 1819 and 1857 to make them more instructional and moral, and other writers worked to create tales more appropriate for children."[114] *Napoleon Dynamite* is an updated fairy tale in its

---

[114]Zipes, *Happily Ever After*, 5.

own right. In a clever line that reinforces Napoleon's complex character as well as provides the moral, Napoleon tells Pedro before he gives his speech, "Pedro, just listen to your heart. That's what I do." This short comment tidily sums the theme illustrated by the famous dance shortly after Pedro's speech. In essence, Napoleon demonstrates just how potent an awkward adolescent's individuality can be. Though he is an immature adolescent who doesn't always make the right decisions in terms of speech or action, Napoleon, through this dance, shows how endearing qualities like loyalty can be rewarded even in the most eccentric of characters. Even though the stage of adolescence[115] is awkward, *Napoleon Dynamite* shows how an anti-hero in a postmodern age can still fulfill a traditional, Cinderella dream, not by conforming or transforming himself to "normal" standards, but by highlighting his individuality in terms of fashion, idiosyncratic gestures and dialogue, and time.

---

[115]In regards to adolescence being an awkward in-between phase, it's interesting that Zipes on page 8 of *Happily Ever After* makes a comment about how the "intersections between so-called children's art and adult art are rarely studied. In fact, it is commonly known, despite substantial achievements in the field, that children's literature is given short shrift at the university as 'kiddie lit,' and it is hardly ever included in popular studies or cultural studies programs." It is my hope that films like *Napoleon Dynamite* can serve as a bridge between these two fields of study and more.

CHAPTER SIX

HARRY THE HERO? THE QUEST FOR SELF-IDENTITY, HEROISM, AND TRANSFORMATION IN THE *GOBLET OF FIRE*

SARA CRABTREE

[Editor's note: The material in this article was originally presented at the 33rd annual conference of the Children's Literature Association, at Manhattan Beach, California, in June 2006.]

When J.K. Rowling unleashed the character of Harry Potter on an unsuspecting audience in 1996, she unknowingly set the stage for one of the most important revolutions in children's literature as well as in the film industry. This series of books has not only intrigued readers by playing toward their sense of mystery, but it has also awakened the imaginations of the young and old alike. *Harry Potter* has become, in essence, a unifying bridge between child and adult as believers in magic, or believers in "the other," whatever that "other" may be.

This monster in the publishing world soon became a giant in the film industry when, in 2002, Daniel Radcliffe charmed his way into the hearts of millions of filmgoers as he learned for the first time that he, Harry Potter, was a wizard, and in fact, had been touted as "the boy who lived." The paradox that Harry Potter would be successful in the book and film industries is not coincidence. J.K. Rowling writes texts that are rich in imagery and play on the educator's knowledge of mythology, history, and literature. This factor, along with the great fantastic images one conjures while reading a Rowling novel and the advancements in film special effects, were destined to be combined into a work of art; hence *Harry Potter and the Sorcerer's Stone*.

The Sorcerer's Stone paved the way for other film giants to lend a hand at bringing Harry Potter to life. Each director had his own way of making Harry Potter a believable character. Following the success of the *Sorcerer's Stone*, a movie which closely followed the Rowling text, subsequent directors were set with a challenge: the longer the book, the more decisions about how closely to follow the text would need to be made. How were the characters going to develop in the movies versus the characters in the books? What events could be cut without losing too much of the storyline? The questions, I am sure, were endless.

With the release of each movie comes the progressional development of the main characters. The characters, to the point that *Goblet of Fire*[116] had been released, remained fairly consistent with the portrayal of the characters in the novels. In *Sorcerer's Stone*, Harry was the innocent, 11 year-old boy who struggled to understand his true identity. In *Chamber of Secrets*, Harry, emboldened with fear that his newfound home would be taken from him, finds loyalty and courage within himself, at least enough to defeat the basilisk and destroy the diary of Tom Riddle. In the *Prisoner of Azkaban*, there is a moment when finally the audience sees a bit of independence and "spark" from Harry. Harry, having been tormented by the dementors the entire film, almost dies trying to rely on someone else to take care of him. Finally, with just a spark of soul left in his body, the other version of Harry Potter, the Harry Potter who has been thwarted back in time with the help of Hermione and her time turner, conjures a patronus charm and defends the real Harry and Sirius Black from eminent death.

The fourth adaptation, *Harry Potter and the Goblet of Fire*, depicts Harry Potter differently from the character that J.K. Rowling created. The portrayal of Harry Potter in the film adaptation challenges audiences to accept Harry as a more mature, capable adolescent, while the novel still hangs on to the idea that Harry Potter is a character in transition, a novice in the wizarding world. The difference between these two portrayals of Harry Potter changes the way in which readers view the role of the Hero. This paper seeks to examine these roles and the differences that exist between the Harry Potter of the novel and the Harry Potter of the film.

Understanding the Hero Archetype

Joseph Campbell said in *The Power of Myth* the reason there are so many stories of the hero in mythology is that "that's worth writing about...[They have] found or done something beyond the normal range of achievement and experience. A hero is who has given his or her life to something bigger than oneself."[117] The fascination with the hero in literature is certainly not a new

---

[116]*Harry Potter and the Goblet of Fire*. dir. Mike Newell, 157 minutes, Warner Brothers, 2005, DVD.
[117]Joseph Campbell and Bill Moyers, *The Power of Myth*. (New York: Doubleday, 1998), 151.

topic for discussion. However, the face of the hero is changing. In classic mythologies, the hero can be described as having

> great—sometimes superhuman—physical strength; they had the gods to intervene for or against them; and in general they never existed as real people. A hero had to have courage, wit, and the will to overcome obstacles. He had to be a good leader and a good father figure to his followers. He would be merciless to enemies but show mercy to the weak. Sometimes he would act with great altruism, that is, on behalf of others without regard for self or self-interest.[118]

This explanation of the classic hero certainly conjures familiar stories for those versed in mythologies. From Hercules in Greek mythology to Moses in the Bible, each hero would have been presented in literature with many of the mentioned qualities. These characters and other more modern characters and stories—such as Neo in the film, *The Matrix*—are part of a human need to "try to come to terms with the world, to harmonize our lives with reality."[119] Humans have long since had the desire to understand how the world around them works. Inherent in our nature is the need to know why we are here, how we got here, and where we go next. Mythologies give us the opportunity to explore various ways of "truths" for these major questions.

The classic hero is an idealistic character that is often inaccessible to readers for the simple fact that most classic heroes are not real. They are the creation of an author or society; their purpose is to teach a lesson, fulfill a quest. While readers may identify with the trials the heroes endure, the quests are often obscure and unimportant to our modern sensibilities. In addition to the obscurity of the task, classic heroes typically boast some great power or strength that sets them apart from ordinary people. For Hercules, it was his strength. For Luke Skywalker, his lineage was enough. Each hero uses his or her extraordinary gift to help him or her complete the tasks. Without these gifts, the hero would be an average, everyday person.

The Modern Hero

To understand the concept of a modern hero, I did what all good teachers do. I asked the students I teach (a motley crew of hoodlums and saints, also known as 6th graders) what a hero was to them. When I posed this question to my students, I had forgotten to think about the fact that this group of kids had grown up in a world at war, one that has been fighting for homeland security and

---

[118]Aileen M. Carroll, "Modern Heroes" *Mythology: A Teaching Unit,*
<http://www.dl.ket.org/latin1/mythology/modernheroes.htm> (22 June 2006).
[119]Campbell and Moyers, Ibid., 2.

antiterrorism for a major portion of their lives. I also failed to recognize these students did not remember a literary world without *Harry Potter*. I admit to these shortcomings in my thinking because they are important to understanding how my concept of a hero and my students' concepts are different because of the world they know. My concept of a hero was a more classical ideal of quests and noble deeds. Heroes that readily flowed off my tongue when asked for an example were characters like King Arthur or Robin Hood. However, my students did not name these characters. For them, these characters were unimportant, and many students had never been exposed to these classic tales.

My students were quick to inform me about who they felt were heroes. Their list, not surprisingly, is a reflection of the world in which they have grown up. On their list of modern heroes they have soldiers, fire-fighters, police officers, and doctors. This list, while not complete, is a good indicator of how the concept of the hero is changing. The hero is becoming more synonymous with the concept of a role model rather than the classic hero. This shift in paradigm is an important one to recognize because every society needs a hero; heroes are important in our lives. In *The Hero with a Thousand Faces*, Campbell says "it has been the prime function of mythology and rite to supply the symbols that carry the human spirit forward."[120] If the symbols that will move our spirits forward are heroes, and I argue there is no better symbol to which we should attach our spirits, then we need to be able discern between types of heroes who will speak to generations in the future as the heroes in classic tales have spoken to us.

Unlike the classic hero, the modern hero does not need an extraordinary gift in order to complete a quest. The modern hero is defined more by the deeds he or she performs rather than the journey he or she undertakes. Modern heroes are personal and random. They are often ordinary people who demonstrate a strong morality in their daily lives. The modern hero stands up for his or her beliefs, fights against injustice, and recognizes small changes help make a big difference in the overall scheme of things. The modern hero has courage when facing danger, but does not boast about always being brave: bravery and boastfulness are attributes best left for those who are inconsiderate of others.

Harry Potter: Classic or Modern Hero?

For the purposes of examining the film adaptation and J.K. Rowling's text, *Harry Potter and the Goblet of Fire,* both definitions of hero—the classic and modern—are important. Harry Potter is written to mirror the classic hero. Each of his adventures completes the archetypal pattern of the hero quest. The stages

---

[120]Joseph Campbell, *The Hero with a Thousand Faces* (New York: Pantheon, 1949), 11.

of the hero quest are the Ordinary World, Call to Adventure, Resistance, Outrage, Commitment to the Journey, Challenge and Adventure, Heart of the Storm, Resurrection and Rebirth, Rewards, and finally Purpose. The following table explains how *Goblet of Fire* completes the stages in Campbell's hero quest.

The Ordinary World	The Dursley's House, London
Call to Adventure	Name pulled from Goblet of Fire
Resistance	"He was sure he was dreaming" (272)
Outrage	"I didn't put my name in" (272)
Committing to the Journey	"Bound to compete in tournament" (277)
Challenge and Adventure	Ron and Harry fight; Everyone supports Cedric
Heart of the Storm	3 challenges
The Resurrection	Confrontation with Voldemort; Return to Hogwarts
The Rewards	Winning the tournament; Telling Voldemort is back
Life Purpose	Mission: Combat Evil—Voldemort

The chart is accurate for both the book and film adaptation with one exception. The Ordinary World is not the Dursleys' House in the film adaptation; instead it is the Weasleys' home. Understanding how the book and movie are constructed around the hero quest helps us to better grasp the idea that Harry is supposed to be accepted as a hero. Harry performs all necessary activities that would identify him as a classic hero.

Because the definition of a hero is shifting, it is important to examine Harry as a modern hero as well as a classic hero. The success of the *Harry Potter* series means that for this generation of children, and subsequent generations, Harry Potter will be looked at as a *typical* hero, which means that children will readily accept the idea that he is a classic hero, if not also a modern one. Because Harry Potter teeters on the fence between this paradigm shift, and because the world in which Harry Potter exists mirrors the world in which these children live (prewar, during war, postwar) the heroes that represent our modern society will carry forward the values with which our human spirits identify.

A Fork in the Road

While J.K. Rowling undoubtedly created Harry Potter to be a classic hero, and he certainly exhibits many of the characteristics we associate with the classic hero, I do not, in fact, believe him to be a classic hero. Nor do I believe

Harry Potter to be a modern hero. Harry Potter, I argue, is not a hero, but he does have the *potential* to become one. Nevertheless, the type of hero Harry will be is neither a classic nor a modern hero. In actuality, the hero that Harry Potter is destined to become is a bittersweet combination of the classic and modern hero. He is a child of destiny who must "face a long period of obscurity. This is a time of extreme danger, impediment, or disgrace. He is thrown inward to his own depths or outward to the unknown; either way, what he touches is a darkness unexplored. And this is a zone of unsuspected presences, benign as well as malignant."[121]   The type of hero Harry Potter will become is the everyman hero. This is a hero that is easily accessible and readily understood by a majority of readers or viewers. Thanks to modern technologies, characters like Harry Potter and J.R.R. Tolkien's hero Aragorn are finding new followers because of their film adaptations. These adaptations make the hero accessible to more people, thus influencing the harmony between life and reality. When we read or view a text, we take part of that story and make it part of our experiences. Our behaviors may change; our intellect is stimulated. We become part of that world as much as it becomes part of ours—at least for a while. When the effect wears off, there is still a lingering feeling of greater understanding. That greater understanding is where the harmony exists.

Because film adaptations allow more people to take part in the experiences of the main characters, the contribution of a film to help move the spirit forward is far greater. The adaptation is a text within itself and presents information differently from the original text. In the case of *Goblet of Fire*, a stronger, more able character is substituted for Harry Potter in the film. The Harry Potter in the novel exists as a character in transition. Because of the different portrayals, the face of the hero changes as necessary. These changes make individually evaluating these two characters important. By looking at the three tasks which occur in both mediums, we can examine both presentations of the Harry Potter character and evaluate his ability to become a hero.

Examining the Adaptation

In the film adaptation of *Goblet of Fire*, we begin to see the sort of activities that will catapult Harry from his reputation as "the boy who lived" to his destiny with heroism. The Harry Potter in this film begins acting more like an independent character rather than a leech who clings to his more capable friend Hermione for magical guidance. In a sense, he begins to become comfortable in his own skin. This Harry Potter is a substitution for the original due to constraints that an adaptation must make. *Goblet of Fire* is a massive book, 734

---

[121]Campbell, *Hero*, 326.

pages, packed with details. Translating this much information to the screen means adapting the story and the characters. The decision to cut many of the events that happen both at the beginning of the novel and in between tasks adds to the focus on Harry becoming a capable wizard in his own right.

Expediting the plot means the characters will need to have enough knowledge to perform the tasks ahead of them; these tasks are part of the Tri-wizard tournament, the competition in which Harry has been entered, though is too young and under-qualified. The tournament consists of the three tasks, each a mini-hero quest in its own right. Also, each task poses danger to the "champions" and requires that each champion defeat the enemy faced if each wishes to advance and win the tournament. Harry faces the same challenges that his older competitors face, though the rules of the game say he is not yet old enough to know what he should in order to compete properly. The level of magic Harry is required to use is a level that stretches his abilities to the thinnest thread. Despite these disadvantages and though he does not want to, Harry accepts the fact that his name was pulled from the goblet and that he must compete in the tournament.

The events leading up to the first task are important in determining what sort of character Harry Potter is. Previous experience with Harry tells us that he is a bit hot-headed and often puts his security in danger to resolve problems most adolescents would gladly let more experienced people handle. While Harry would have been glad to let the older students engage in competition, that choice was taken from him when his name came out of the goblet. Harry does, however, keep his hot-headed spirit about him as the first task approaches. Harry and Ron have an argument, and Harry refuses to talk to Ron. Harry's sense of self is extremely strong in the scenes where he and Ron bicker. He refuses to admit wrongdoing, though Ron's jealousy and feelings of inadequacy weigh heavily on him. Ron's loyalty does not waiver, despite his jealousy towards Harry, and Ron sends Harry to visit Hagrid (in a round-about way). It is Harry's visit with Hagrid that reveals the first task, the dragons. Having this information could have set Harry apart from the other champions, but Harry chooses to even the playing field.

Instead of keeping the information about the dragons to himself, and despite the growing dislike of Harry as the Hogwarts Champion (playing against Cedric Diggory), Harry decides he must share the information with his fellow schoolmate. Sharing this information shows a quality the other champions lack—integrity. Harry does not attempt to play the game in an unfair manner. He knows the other two schools competing will have the information, and keeping knowledge of the dragons to himself would make him feel as if he were cheating in a sense. Though he might cheat on his homework, Harry knows this task is more important than the mundane school work that he repeatedly chooses not to complete because if he or any of the champions fail to do well, they could die. Harry shares with Cedric because in his extraordinary life, he has found something inside himself, what Roni Natov calls "the strength to do the right thing, to establish a moral code."[122]

The moral code that Harry exhibits before the tasks begin stems from the tragic life he has lead. If the death of his parents was not enough of a tragedy for a baby to deal with, then certainly being raised by "hostile relatives" is. The combination of events that occur early in Harry's life and the almost inhumane way he is treated by the Dursleys helps him understand that he is a child who is "on [his] own, unacknowledged, unappreciated, unseen, and unheard, up against an unfair parent, and by extension, an unfair world. Justice and the lack of it reign supreme."[123] Harry's sense of injustice is amplified by his experiences. His one defense against such inequity is to exhibit his integrity, which he does by sharing his knowledge to help prepare Cedric.

The First Task

In the film adaptation, the first task comes very quickly. The tournament is the main focus of the film, and many of the lessons Harry learns in the novel are not present in film. Though the tournament has been limited to wizards who have more experience than Harry, the film has a quiet undertone that almost shouts, "Harry is experienced enough." With the exception of Dumbledore's outburst right after Harry is chosen as champion, it seems the students at Hogwarts are afraid that Harry will take the spotlight away from Cedric. This fear is a reaction to Harry's behavior in the previous three films. Perhaps as the students grow older, their resentment for the "boy who lived" also grows. It's not that Harry Potter is an exceptionally talented wizard, but that his multiple brushes with danger keep him in the limelight.

The first task begins in the belly of the whale, the place Campbell in *The Hero with a Thousand Faces* calls "the magical threshold" in which the hero will "transit into a sphere of rebirth."[124] This belly, the tent which serves as a waiting area for the champions, is the place where each of the champions must come to terms with who they are as a wizard. It is in this tent that nerves and emotions could get the best of each champion, and each champion could decide to combat the dragon with a strategy that is not successful. The minute the curtain parts, the champion needs to be sure of his strategy, and ready to fight. Harry has been coached by Mad Eye Moody, who asks pointedly "Now, what

---

[122]Roni Natov, "Harry Potter and the Extraordinariness of the Ordinary," *The Lion and the Unicorn* 25,no.2 (2001), 323.
[123]Ibid., 310, 311.
[124]Campbell, *Hero*, 90.

are you going to do about your dragon?" After Harry stumbles with his words, and is not able to answer the question, Moody suggests that each of the other three champions will have a strategy to defeat the dragon that would play to his or her strength. Harry must decide what his strengths are, and how he can best use them to win this challenge.

One must quietly giggle at the idea of Harry and his strengths. Harry, up to this point, has shown a strong aptitude for getting caught doing whatever off-color activity he has deemed necessary. He has also shown the ability to be a little "cheeky" with his peers. Most of all, he has shown that he likes to fight against things he believes are unjust. Finally, Harry declares, "I can fly. I am a fair flyer," to which Moody responds, "better than fair the way I hear it." At this moment Harry embraces his abilities. He does not pretend he is good at spells or potions. Instead, Harry accepts the advice of his newfound mentor, enters the cave, and prepares to emerge as the champion he believes himself to be. As a result, Harry defeats the dragon after demonstrating top-notch Quidditch-style flying. His defensive maneuvers help readers to understand that Harry's skills are physical, not mental. If Harry is going to become any kind of hero, the physical is the area in which Harry will have to prove his proficiency.

The Second Task

The second task begins the moment Harry and the other champions retrieve the golden egg from the dragon. First they must figure out what the task is and then figure out how to complete the task. This second task is particularly important for this study because it allows viewers to see Harry making decisions on his own without the advice or aid of his friends. In order for Harry to become a hero, he must learn how to do things on his own. Ultimately, Harry's final challenge of the book series, the challenge he has been training for since he stepped onto the grounds at Hogwarts, is one in which he will battle Lord Voldemort. J.K. Rowling has foreshadowed that either Harry or Voldemort will die in the end, so this challenge is one which Harry will face alone. In every other task or deed Harry can have help, but if we will ever see Harry as a hero, that last, most important task must be completed without help. Campbell says in the *Power of Myth,* "If you have someone who can help you, that's fine, too. But, ultimately, the last deed has to be done by oneself."[125]   While it's acceptable for Harry to accept the help from his peers for other challenges, defeating Voldemort alone will be no easy battle. Harry must be able to think and act quickly and without regret if he wishes to defeat the ultimate challenge. And Harry, it seems, is always up for a challenge.

---

[125]Campbell and Moyer, *Power,* 184.

Regarding the second task of the Tri-Wizard tournament, the obstacles which Harry must overcome in this challenge are more conducive to being solved alone. The first obstacle, figuring out what the screeching gold egg means, is solved using a tip from Cedric and encouragement from an unlikely source, Moaning Myrtle. Together, the information these two characters provide helps Harry to discover that something important to him has been taken, and is being held captive by the Merpeople at the bottom of the Black Lake. His challenge is to get back what is important to him, and he only has an hour to do it. But how does one survive at the bottom of a lake for an hour? To solve his problem, Harry enlists the help of Ron and Hermione. Together the three search the library for any spell, plant, or charm that would allow Harry to breathe underwater. However, once again, help comes from an unlikely source. Neville Longbottom comes to Harry's rescue and shares with him a plant that will allow him to breathe.

At this point, the task belongs to Harry alone. Without incident, Harry makes it to the bottom of the lake and sees both Ron and Hermione, along with two others, being held captive by the Merpeople. Harry notices the time is short and makes a decision to free the captives. The Merpeople tell him no, but Harry persists, aggressively fighting against something he has decided is unjust. For Harry, the lives of the innocent people trapped at the bottom of the lake are more important than his own life. He does not seem concerned about winning, but rather about the endangered people, putting his life and the tournament at stake to do what he feels is right. In other words, Harry's intuition tells him what is more important: his friends.

When Harry makes the decision to put other people's needs ahead of his own, he lives up to a statement he makes earlier in the film when he says to Ron, "I don't want fame; I want to be normal." Saving the lives of people certainly does not categorize Harry as normal, but losing the challenge proves his head is in the right place. Harry is promptly rewarded for his deed underwater when Dumbledore declares Harry tied for second place because of his "outstanding moral character."

This moral character Harry is purported to have is the type of characteristic that has become a staple for the type of hero expected in our society today, the type of hero my students expect to see in film and literature. It is this Harry Potter who faces extreme danger but uses what he knows to overcome certainty of death that my students can identify with, the kind of hero that is accessible to many, especially in the face of war. This hero reconciles his belief of what is right with his longing to win and still comes out on top. Ultimately, this is the hero who gives hope to those in tough circumstances.

The Third Task

The third task is the most unimpressive task in the film adaptation because solving the maze and finding the trophy in the center is too similar to many of the other tasks Harry defeated when he was younger, like in Harry's first year when he defeated the Wizard's Chess game. This maze requires the same type of skills in which Harry's physical and mental abilities could shine more so than his magical abilities. Most notably, solving the maze requires quick decisions and intuition; Harry requires no help, though Moody directs Harry in which way to go.

The maze is riddled with a number of obstacles, including a bewitched champion, Victor Krum, who attacks another champion. Nevertheless, Harry shows his moral fiber throughout the competition in the maze until he is just feet from the trophy. When Cedric is overtaken by the bushes, Harry becomes torn between helping him or winning the tournament. Once again, Harry lets his sense of integrity make the choice. He frees Cedric, and together they race to the cup. Harry is content to share the glory with Cedric, but there won't be any. This decision seals Cedric's fate; Cedric will die.

The most interesting part of this maze challenge in the film adaptation is the battle between Harry and Voldemort in the graveyard. In this battle, Harry once again shows integrity by telling Cedric to go back. If Cedric had chosen to and been successful in returning, Harry would have been left alone to fight Voldemort without a way back. However, Cedric's choice is cut short, and he is killed. Once Voldemort is resurrected, he and Harry battle. Ironically, while in battle, Harry is helped by another unlikely source, the spirits of the last few people Voldemort had killed, which included his parents. It is important to remember that Harry does not use magic beyond his years in this scene, but instead, with pure courage, Harry manages to escape from Voldemort and return to Hogwarts.

Though Harry's battle with Voldemort is short this time, we know he will eventually battle Voldemort for the ultimate win. When Harry returns to Hogwarts, he declares through tears, "He's back. He's back. Voldemort is back." This moment of weakness is another indication that Harry is capable of becoming a hero. He feels the loss of life, the death of a friend, and the trauma of survivor's guilt when people around you always seem to die. While he could choose not to feel these things and instead remain dark and dubious, he doesn't. Instead, Harry embraces his feelings and chooses good, despite the emotional pain it brings.

Examining the Novel

While the adaptation stays fairly consistent to the portrayal of Harry Potter in the novel, there are substantial differences surrounding each of the tasks that make the two versions quite different from each other. These differences reinforce the idea that Harry Potter in the film is a stronger, more capable character than the Harry in the book. In the novel, we still see Harry as a character-in-progress. It's clear Harry needs to mature more, to let adolescence take its toll on him. Furthermore, it is more apparent in the novel that Harry is still struggling to accept his fate, while the Harry in the adaptation has already accepted his.

The First Task

The days leading up to the first task reveal Harry's squeamishness towards the upcoming challenge. He is almost un-composed, distraught, and frightful. Knowing about the dragons seems to throw Harry out of balance. In the previous novels, Harry fought beasts that were just as scary as the dragons. Defeating the troll was no easy task, but one Harry accomplished. What about the Spiders? Harry managed to escape them as well. The difference between those previous tasks and this one seems to be *knowledge*. Harry thinks to himself that "he didn't know whether he was glad he'd seen what was coming or not. Perhaps this way was better. The first shock was over now." But the *shock* of the task seems to be what is throwing Harry off. This becomes more apparent when "Harry got up on Sunday morning and dressed so inattentively that it was a while before he realized he was trying to pull his hat onto his foot instead of his sock."[126] Nerves have obviously gotten the better of Harry. This is not the same confident Harry of the film; this Harry is scared.

When Harry approaches Cedric to share with him the information about the dragons, Harry avoids the crowds who have been taunting him. This behavior is unlike the behavior of Harry in the film, who did not like the teasing, but still purposefully had a clear mission. Instead, Harry in the novel is a bit of a coward, avoiding people to make his life easier. After Harry shares the news of the dragons with Cedric, he sees "some of the panic he'd been feeling."[127] Are these the behaviors of a hero? Is this the kind of person we wish to defend us? Is this the kind of character we identify with? While bravery is not an attribute one should always display, Harry lacks any bravery or courage in these scenes,

---

[126] J.K. Rowling, *Harry Potter and the Goblet of Fire* (New York: Scholastic, 2000), 329, 337.
[127] Ibid., 341.

and having the courage to face difficult situations like these should be an attribute a hero would have.

Another major difference between the novel's portrayal of the first task and the film's adaptation is the amount of help Harry receives in preparation to face the dragon. Harry in the film seems to have a keen grasp on the spells and techniques he needs in order to get past the dragon; however, in the novel Hermione has to teach Harry how to do a proper summoning spell to call his broom from the castle, without which he could not have gotten past the dragon and retrieved the egg. This difference lets viewers of the film see Harry as a more gifted wizard with more abilities than he actually has.

The Second Task

The differences that exist between the film and the novel for the second task are similar to those in the first. The adaptation chooses to change the way Harry is given aid in order to project him as a more capable wizard. In both versions, Harry sneaks into the prefects' bathroom to unravel the mystery of the egg with the aid of Moaning Myrtle. When Harry figures out he must swim to the bottom of the Black Lake within an hour to retrieve something of importance to him, he is faced with the possibility of death. How is he to hold his breath for that length of time? Harry asks Myrtle, "'how am I supposed to breathe?'"[128] Myrtle leaves this problem for Harry to figure out on his own. But, true to Harry's abilities, he can't figure out this problem on his own and turns to Hermione and Ron for help.

Together, the three of them venture into the library to search for something that would allow Harry to breathe underwater for an extended period of time. The search is unsuccessful, and the morning of the challenge Harry is still perplexed as to how he will manage the task. On that morning, Harry is awakened by Dobby, the house elf, who informs him that "'Harry Potter needs to hurry. . . the second task starts in ten minutes.'" Harry reveals his defeatist attitude and declares, "'It's too late Dobby. . . I'm not doing the task, I don't know how.'"[129] Harry is rescued by Dobby who shoves a wad of gilleyweed into his hands, telling him he must do the task to save Ron. When Harry discovers that Ron is the item the Merpeople are holding captive, he finds enough courage to participate.

The film adaptation, once again, shows Harry to be more astute than the novel. In the film, it was Neville who rescued Harry by supplying him with the gilleyweed. However, Harry did not whine about his inabilities. Instead, he

---

[128]Ibid., 465.
[129]Ibid., 490.

continued to search and explore his resources, never declaring his incapability. This Harry, again, demonstrates what a hero is more so than Harry in the novel.

The Third Task

Harry's performance in the third task of the novel looks much like the one in the film. He needs no help from others to solve the maze. One small difference between the two versions is that in the novel, Moody does not assist Harry with directions. The maze of the novel has more creatures and obstacles to overcome, but Harry has faced them all before. The integrity that Harry shows after helping Cedric stays true in both versions as well.

However, the difference between the novel and film comes in the graveyard after Harry and Cedric are transported by the portkey. In the novel, they both get their bearings and then ready their wands. In the film, Harry instructs Cedric to get back to the portkey, knowing that sending Cedric back would mean sacrificing himself. Self-sacrifice is a noble attribute, and one that is used to showcase the difference between the two Harrys. While the Harry of the novel desires the companionship that Cedric represents, the Harry of the film knows Cedric represents innocence. Dragging an innocent person into battle against Voldemort is something Harry would never do. Harry intuits that he alone will face Voldemort in the end, so his desire to send Cedric back is a most heroic quality.

Final Comments

While I argue that neither version of Harry is a hero to this point, I do see the potential for Harry to become what he is destined to be. Harry wants to protect the magical world where he has found comfort and acceptance, and for the first time in his life, he recognizes a family as his own. The magic world Harry has become a part of has offered him a refuge the muggle world never could. It's in this world that Harry must grow up and prepare himself for the final battle between Voldemort and himself. Because Harry is still a character in progress and the last novel has not been released yet, we do not yet know the fate of Harry. Many questions still lay heavily on the shoulders of J.K Rowling as she completes the series.

Harry Potter certainly has some connections between the children I turned to while examining the role of a hero in our society. Like Harry, these children have grown up in a time of war. The war that preceded Harry's birth is similar to the Gulf war that preceded the birth of many of my students. And like Harry, my students find themselves with relatives who have been killed serving and protecting their country. *Goblet of Fire* shows the beginning of a war whose hopeful victor will be Harry Potter.

The success of Harry Potter, both film and novel versions, is explained by Bill Moyers in Campbell's *The Power of Myth*. Moyers, in a discussion about the success of the *Star Wars* films declares, "it came along at a time when people needed to see in recognizable images the clash of good and evil. They needed to be reminded of idealism, to see a romance based upon selflessness rather than selfishness."[130] For this generation, Harry Potter is the recognizable clash of good and evil. Harry will grow up battling forces that are beyond him, yet he will always overcome adversity. He has to have the potential to become more than a mediocre wizard. It's that potential that readers identify with, and it's that potential that allows us to reconcile our reality with our humanity.

---

[130]Campbell and Moyers, *Power*, 177.

CONCLUSION

LANCE WELDY

As I sit here in Kiel, Germany, finalizing this book, I find myself confident in the appropriateness of its title. The chapters serve as a great representative of a diverse group of contributors as well as a diverse choice of text and textual analyses. Throughout this book, these scholars have discussed and analyzed issues surrounding colonialism, identity and conformity, and intertextuality; but the thread that holds these topics together is Transformation, and it is this transformative perspective in Children's Literature that still remains a topic to be researched in different ways.

What have we learned in terms of this whole theme of Transformation? For the purposes of this book, we have used Transformation to demonstrate the powerful post-colonial rejection of hegemony, the shifting representation of African-American children in 1930s American Literature, the phenomenon behind the child as a colonized subject, as well as the refutation of conformity in a high school setting. As a response to these historical and oppressive ideas of conformity and colonialism, the authors in this book have chosen to reveal the impact of intertextuality and postmodernism in Children's / Youth Literature. Transformation in these elements is evident, especially in how this book approaches concepts such as format, the use of theatrical expression and scenic aesthetics, and the fairy tale and quest motif. All in all, this book more than adequately introduces and highlights relevant topics surrounding and intersecting with the concept of Transformation.

But this book never set out to be an exhaustive analysis of Transformation in Children's / Youth Literature. Part of the beauty of academic inquiry is the inherent potential for research beyond the originally compiled anthology, which could take other scholars into directions hitherto unanticipated. In other words, this collection of essays, when viewed as a whole, lends itself to research questions that may not have formed had the individual parts not been combined. What I want to propose briefly before closing are topics and direction for further research.

For example, Beth Cooley's article on updated biblical typology provides an interesting insight into Lance Weldy's article on the updated Cinderella story. The juxtaposition of these two essays brings about questions for further research, such as, "What are common elements between a Christ-like figure and a Cinderella figure, and how does the concept of Transformation factor into both?" Connected to this question could be one of gender, notably, "How does Stargirl's gender influence the effectiveness of both a Cinderella and typological story?" Furthermore, on a larger scale, how does this idea of Transformation interact or metamorphose, especially as the quintessential prototype for a rags-to-riches story? And could Stargirl's resurrection/transformation be said to equal Napoleon's, or negatively mirror it, especially because her return to the school is as a conventionally "normal" girl? These are just a few questions revolving around these two connected essays.

Likewise, Elina Druker's discussion about spatiality in regards to tactile and material qualities in picture books lends itself to a wide range of topics to explore. Since Druker has established Tove Jansson as a precursor to the postmodern picture book movement, how might Jansson factor into the American picture book scene with such figures as Maurice Sendak, Eric Carle, David Macauley, or Jan Brett? And how has Jansson both adhered to and diverged from the Caldecott tradition? Tammy Mielke's essay could lead to similar questions, not only with the Caldecott tradition and how the African American child is being colonized in both image and text, but also in relation to what kinds of messages are being conveyed through the combination of image and text, and how that combination might clash between authorial intentionality versus illustrator intentionality. Furthermore, how has that representation of the African American child progressed since the 1930s?

Sara Crabtree focuses on two different texts in an on-going series. When the Harry Potter series is finally completed—both the book and the film—how can we then as a whole discuss the transformative nature of this series in connection to classical mythology? How will the ending change or solidify our views about Harry as hero or average Joe? As Lance Weldy's article mentioned several times, a text as recent and alternative as *Napoleon Dynamite* remains untapped and screams for a scholarly critical edition, covering such topics as the root of its rhetorical attraction and reader response theories.

As Mitts-Smith notes in her essay, each of Pennart's book transforms "one former enemy in fairy tales and pits it against another traditional fairy tale enemy." This has actually been a trend in the postmodern era that I would love to pursue as an academic study sometime. What other stereotypical enemies can be updated in the vein of Gregory Maguire's novels like *Wicked* and *Confessions of an Ugly Stepsister*? If we perhaps connected Mitts-Smith's essay to Crabtree's, could we see a potential audience for a future novel or form of criticism employing Snape's point of view, or, better yet, Malfoy's? If postmodernism accepts and encourages the blurring of boundaries and scrutinizing the audience preconception of protagonist vs. antagonist, then certainly these kinds of research questions are valid ones.

Finally, one broad statement about future research questions—We believe that this book will draw an audience from across disciplinary boundaries, such as academics from the fields of Children's and Youth Literature, American and British Literature, Postcolonial and World Literature, and Popular Culture and Film Studies. Because of this, we hope that future research questions will also include avenues conducive to interdisciplinary inquiry. To incorporate Mitts-Smith's usage of Gianni Rodari's "notion of a 'new key' where for instance, one tells the same story in a different time or place or from a different point of view,"[131] I believe that it is feasible not only to see Harry Potter's story sympathetically told from Malfoy's point of view, but also to find Transformative (and connecting) elements in other fields of inquiry. Among other things, this connection will further bolster the credibility of Children's Literature inquiry within the Academy. After all, intertextuality is not a respecter of persons, but is, in actuality, tied to all forms of texts, both in print and visual, and as such, should be made accessible through analyses by scholars in all fields from all corners of the world.

---

[131]Gianni Rodari, *The Grammar of Fantasy* trans. Jack Zipes (New York: Teachers & Writers Collaborative, 1996), 51-52.

CONTRIBUTING AUTHORS

Sara Crabtree is a Ph.D. student in English at the Department of Literature and Languages at Texas A&M-Commerce. She also teaches reading in Garland, Texas. She fell in love with children's literature when she began to teach it. However, *Harry Potter* has been a favorite escape since the early days of grad school when reading for fun was unheard of.

Beth Cooley is the author of two Young Adult novels: *Ostrich Eye*, winner of the 2002 Delacorte Prize, and *Shelter*, also published by Delacorte. She teaches literature and writing at Gonzaga University in Spokane, Washington.

Elina Druker is employed as a teacher and doctoral student at the Department of Literature and History of Ideas at Stockholm University. She is currently working on her dissertation which discusses specific features of the avant-garde picture book in the 1950's. Elina is coordinator and core group member in the Nordic Network for Children's Literature Research and has contributed essays to several Nordic and international publications dealing with children's literature and picture book aesthetics.

Tammy Mielke is a visiting assistant professor at Western Michigan University in Kalamazoo, Michigan, where she teaches children's literature and multicultural adolescent literature. Recently she submitted her Ph.D. thesis, *Literary Constructs of African American Childhood in the 1930s in American Children's Literature* to the University of Worcester in England. Her additional research includes graphic novels as literature for young adults. She also serves as a co-editor for the Children's Literature Association's Newsletter.

Debra Mitts-Smith is a PhD candidate in the Graduate School of Library and Information Science at the University of Illinois at Urbana-Champaign. She is on the faculty of Library and Information Science at Dominican University. Her dissertation is on the visual image of the wolf in children's books, and her research interests include children's and young adult literature, comparative children's literature, the history of the book, and visual literacy and illustration.

Lance Weldy is a 2006-2007 Fulbright Fellow Junior Lecturer in the Center for North American Studies at the Johann Wolfgang Goethe-Universität in Frankfurt am Main, Germany. His areas of specialization are American and Children's literature, with an emphasis on pioneer literature as well as the topic of Transformation in various forms, including media/film. His first monograph under contract, *Seeking a Felicitous Space: The Dialectics of Women and Frontier Space in* Giants in the Earth, Little House on the Prairie, *and* My Ántonia, is through *ibidem*-Verlag.

APPENDIX A

	Setting	Plot		Characters	
Characteristics of Folk or Fairy Tales	"Once upon a time in a place far away"	Conflict--Good vs. Evil	Ending is Happy	Universal--simple, flat, almost stock characters	Seldom undergo internal change
Napoleon Dynamite	Blurring of time, cultural artifacts, rural unidentifiable setting	Napoleon vs. Summer, possibly Uncle Rico as secondary villain	Chapter 19 on DVD is entitled "Happy Ending"; Napoleon and Deb play tetherball	Napoleon is the universal nerd in all of us; Yet an antihero	Napoleon doesn't change; He makes the audience come to him

APPENDIX B

Appendix B
Taken from Donna Norton's Through the Eyes of a Child

	French Perrault's "Cinderella"	German Grimm's "Aschenputtel"	American "Napoleon Dynamite"
Origin			
Cause of Lowly Positions	Mother died. Father remarried.	Mother died. Father remarried.	Appearance? Parents missing. Grandmother present, but doesn't impart best social skills
Outward Signs of Lowly Position	Sitting in ashes. Vilest household tasks.	Wears clogs; old dress. Sleeps in cinders. Heavy work.	Pitted against Uncle Rico and Chip; Ridiculed about no job; forced to feed Tina, the llama
Cinderella's Relationship to Household	Stepdaughter to cruel woman. Unkind stepsisters.	Stepdaughter to cruel woman. Cruel step-sisters.	Considered a child/baby, doesn't have a job
How She Receives Wishes	Wishes to fairy godmother.	Wishes to bird on tree on mother's grave.	He doesn't receive wishes; he's an anti-hero and performs his own agency, draws picture of Trisha and gets a date.
What Keeps Her from Social Occasion	(Ball) No gown. Family won't let her go.	(Ball) Must separate lentils.	1)School Dance—Uncle Rico leaves him stranded, Trisha humiliates him; 2)Student Body Speech—wins over school
Where She Meets the Prince	Castle ball. Beautifully dressed.	Castle ball. Beautifully dressed.	Not applicable
Test of Rightful Cinderella	Glass slipper.	Gold slipper.	Unique Individuality—his dance routine
What Happens to Stepsisters	Forgiven. Live in palace. Marry lords.	Blinded by birds.	Uncle Rico reunited with girlfriend; Kip leaves with LaFawnduh